FIGHT THE GOOD FIGHT

Catherine Fox is not your typical martial artist. Her initiation into the sacred rites of judo began not in a dojo but in the Tunnel Cement Works in Pitstone, Buckinghamshire. And her dedication to the sport has been questionable: a thirty-year sabbatical, two children and a life spent writing books does not prepare one for enlightenment, or for beating your opponent on a padded mat. However, Catherine has set herself a challenge: before she turns forty-five she will become a black belt. After all, how many other vicar's wives get to roll around on the floor with sweaty blokes?

CATHERINE FOX

FIGHT THE GOOD FIGHT

From Vicar's Wife to Killing Machine

Complete and Unabridged

ULVERSCROFT
Leicester

First published in Great Britain in 2007 by
Yellow Jersey
The Random House Group Limited
London

First Large Print Edition
published 2008
by arrangement with
The Random House Group Limited
London

British Library CIP Data

Fox, Catherine, *1961* –
   Fight the good fight: from vicar's wife to killing
machine.—Large print ed.—
   Ulverscroft large print series: non-fiction
   1. Fox, Catherine, *1961* – 2. Judo 3. Women martial
artists—Great Britain—Biography 4. Martial artists
—Great Britain—Biography 5. Spouses of clergy—
Great Britain—Biography 6. Large type books
   I. Title
   796.8′152′092

   ISBN 978–1–84782–324–3

01 |16

Published by
F. A. Thorpe (Publishing)
Anstey, Leicestershire

Set by Words & Graphics Ltd.
Anstey, Leicestershire
Printed and bound in Great Britain by
T. J. International Ltd., Padstow, Cornwall

This book is printed on acid-free paper

For Jonathan and Tom,
who got me back into Judo

Introduction

This is a sports book for the frankly unsporty, for the hapless amateur whose urgent question is not 'How will my intercostals hold up in training today?' so much as 'Does my bum look big in these cycling shorts?' It's for people who have always been a bit useless at sport, who are constantly meaning to lose a bit of weight and get a grip on their lives. It is also for anyone who knows deep down that they are bone idle, but who is nevertheless prepared — when push comes to shove — to lie on the sofa and read a book on the subject.

I'm going to tread carefully in this introduction, because I'm acutely aware that I am labouring under the twin handicaps of martial arts and the Church of England. Both of these worlds appear extremely odd, even frightening, to the outsider. They are full of arcane rituals and language and peopled by eccentrics who wear funny clothes and bow all the time. But here the similarities end. It is only in one of these worlds that someone is likely to approach you without warning and chop you viciously in the kidneys. This will generally turn out to be because you've sat in their pew. In judo, of course, there is no chopping. Judo means 'The Gentle Way'. (That's an example of the famous Japanese sense of humour.)

Why judo?, you may be wondering. There must be other ways for a flabby middle-aged clergy wife to get back into shape. True — but let's be honest here: when it comes to getting fit, the problem most of us face is that we hate physical exercise. If it weren't for the whole business of flailing about getting sweaty and out of breath, we'd be up for it. But who wants to feel like the fat useless one who has to run round the track again because they came in last? Especially now there's no nasty-minded PE teacher (smug in a warm tracksuit) making you do it. Surely the whole point of being a grown-up is that you can skive off games for the rest of your life?

Most of us cave at some stage and re-enter the grubby world of PE. Some people wake up one morning and resolve to run an ironman triathlon. We need not concern ourselves with nutters like that. Ordinary people join a gym. And because they are ordinary, they go three times, then spend the rest of the year comfort-eating to stave off their guilt. Admit it: gyms *are boring*.

This is where judo comes into its own. Judo is not boring, it is endlessly varied. It builds up both strength and stamina. It's good for self-defence. It hones the reflexes, it trains you mentally. It increases your flexibility, it toughens you up. And let's face it, we vicar's wives don't get many opportunities to roll around the floor with a dozen sweaty blokes, so we must take our fun where we can.

The other thing is this: I'm ultra-competitive. I'm also a monumentally bad loser, a combination which brings me grief. I've learned over the years to disguise both these unattractive traits. I don't wear spiked running shoes for the Mums' Race on Sports Day. I don't burst into noisy tears if my sons fail to win the fancy dress competition in World Book Week, even though we are *clearly* the best and were blatantly stitched up by the head teacher.

Here, once again, judo comes into its own. On the mat my competitiveness becomes an asset rather than a liability. If I simply wanted to keep fit, I could join an exercise class, or do a little light housework. Or even some gardening, which is basically just housework, only outdoors with mud and earwigs. (Having said that, this would be a pretty accurate description of our hallway last time I looked.) It is possible to inject an element of competition into domestic chores, but competitive baking and window-cleaning can get so ugly.

No, for me it has to be judo every time. You just can't beat a good grapple with a willing partner. As the actress said to the bishop. (You may have wondered why the paths of bishops so often seem to intersect with members of the acting profession. There is nothing untoward going on, it is simply because bishops are frequently invited to become theatre chaplains, so they just pop in whenever something comes up. As the actress, etc, etc.)

My career trajectory in judo has been a little erratic. I did it for a year as a child, then took thirty years off. When I returned to the sport I vowed that I would be a black belt by the time I was forty-five. I made it my mission to discover what I'm really made of, what my toughness-to-wimp ratio actually is. To tell the truth, I had no real idea. Despite all my bouts of über-competitiveness (whether that be in the sharp-elbowed realm of bargain-hunting, or in a record-breaking nit-combing attempt), I totally failed to take part in any organised sport between the ages of twelve and forty. This quest was the first genuine sporting challenge I had set myself since our school tried to beat Cheddington Primary at netball when I was eleven.

Another reason for setting this goal was to see whether judo has any role to play in the life of a nice, educated middle-class forty-something mother-of-two in the West Midlands. A single young person may be able to drop everything and attach him- or herself to a dojo in Tokyo and train like a psychopath. My story, by contrast, is a sporting quest mired down in everyday life. I have to juggle training with all my other commitments — on top of ironing clerical shirts, remembering where the PE kits are and shouting at people to empty the dishwasher and feed the guinea pigs. (Before emptying the dishwasher and feeding the guinea pigs.)

This pilgrimage will be enhanced, I hope, by my own distinctive soundtrack — the smash hits from *Hymns Ancient and Modern*. (Or, if we're being pedantic, *Hymns Ancient and Even More Ancient*.) I had a deprived childhood. My parents never bought a television, so I grew up knowing hymns the way normal children knew pop songs. As a youngster, I felt this keenly as a disadvantage, but as time (like an ever-rolling stream) has gone on, I have come to consider myself fortunate. There is not a single situation in life for which I have no appropriate hymn to cheer the soul. Or annoy people, let's not deny it. A well-timed rendition of the old temperance hymn 'Have courage, my boy, to say 'no'!' never fails with teenage lads.

It is my sincere hope and prayer that this quest will turn me into a better person: more gentle, more balanced, full of self-control, integrity and honesty. And what better way to commence than by admitting that the above statement is a big fat lie? The real reason is simple: I want a black belt because it puts the fear of God into people. And — watch my scary eyes — I'm going to get one. I'm sick of being a weakling, and having twenty-stone bullies kick fairy cakes into my face at the church bazaar. Stand aside, mortals. No more Mrs Nice Vicar's wife. Here comes the killing machine.

1

White Belt

Fight the good fight with all thy might,
Christ is thy strength, and Christ thy right;
Lay hold on life, and it shall be
Thy joy and crown eternally.

*Verse 1, Hymn 54, 'Fight the Good Fight',
in With Cheerful Voice: Hymns for
Children (Words Edition)*

My First Fights

If you went to an English primary school in
the sixties and seventies, you may still be able
to visualise the cover of this book, with
its bold green and turquoise ripples and
white writing. You may even remember the
satisfying smack it made when you 'accidentally' dropped it on the hall floor in assembly,
just after the headmaster had said, 'Hands
together and eyes closed.' I was never a
book-dropper myself — I was only five at the

height of that particular craze, but I secretly wanted to be.

I doubt we ever thought about the words of 'Fight the Good Fight'. It was many years before it was anything more to me than one of the things you sang in school assembly, and nowhere else, along with 'When a Knight won his Spurs'. We were given instructions about how to sing it: 'Lay hold on life, — *breathe!* — and it shall be-ee — *All in one breath now, children, there's no comma, carry on to the next line* — eee Thy joy and crowni-ter-ner-leeee!' (corporate whoop of air being sucked into collapsing lungs).

Even so, I expect I would have been able to make a distinction between 'the *good* fight' (i.e. being a Christian) and 'the *bad* fight' (the kind we had in the playground). Fighting was not in any way countenanced at Brookmead County Primary School. This meant you had to be quick. There were only ever a few moments before the gathered crowd chanting 'Bun-*dle*! Bun-*dle*!' drew the attention of teachers or dinner ladies, who promptly put a stop to it.

There were many different types of playground fight; scraps, bullying, kick-and-run incidents, punch-ups and the semi-organised mayhem which is British bulldog. British bulldog was banned at our school, so instead we played a game called 'mush', which is completely unlike British bulldog, in the sense that you spell it differently. These days, to our horrified disbelief, the stakes are sometimes very high indeed. Children bring knives into school. There are fatal stabbings in corridors or outside the gates. We look back to the innocent scuffles of our schooldays and think how different it all was back then. Maybe it was. But maybe the difference today lies in the availability of lethal weapons and the reluctance of the adult population to confront other people's children, rather than in some kind of lost innocence.

It's easy to forget, as adults, the sheer, unadulterated, murderous rage a child can feel. 'Oops,' we say, exchanging private grins with other parents as the toddler flings herself about the sitting-room floor. 'We seem to be having a bit of a paddy!' We agree to take no notice, to be completely unmoved so as not to reward that kind of behaviour. She'll grow out of it. She's got to learn. All that fuss over a chocolate biscuit! Yes, but call to mind how it felt to be so thwarted and so impotent. An angry toddler will inflict as much damage as it physically can. Usually, of course, this is not very much. The theory is that self-control will develop alongside physical strength, so that the child will never have a truly disastrous combination of unbridled rage and potency.

Now and then one gets away. I remember a werewolf moment when I was about ten: a fight in Miss Finch's classroom one playtime with another group of girls. One of them bashed me in the face, right over the nose, with a big stick. Everything went dark red. My lips peeled back from my teeth and the hair on my head stood up and my hands reached out like claws, surging with wicked strength. I grabbed the upper arms of the first enemy I came upon and dug my rigid fingers in. Afterwards, when I came to, I felt shocked and a bit sick. The following day my victim had bruises, four fingers and a thumb, on each arm. Why I didn't get into trouble, I shall never know. If my sons came home marked like that I'd be up at the school in a second. I spent days braced and fearful, but nothing ever happened.

By a strange series of coincidences I met my victim again, twenty-five years later, and was able to apologise. She couldn't remember a thing about it, but sportingly went ahead and forgave me anyway. Oddly enough, we had both ended up as vicars' wives, and it all seemed a bit ridiculous. I mean, vicars' wives would no more go about pinching people than we'd gob in the communion wine. It was just a silly school-girl spat. Now and then I ask myself if was it just luck that my hands closed on her arms and not round her throat. Surely even in my rage I knew better than to throttle another girl, especially a younger one.

So. I was nasty horrid pinching girl. Pinching isn't as bad as biting, but it's pretty bad. Pinching is spiteful. It's *girl* fighting, along with hair-pulling and faceslapping and scratching. I hardly ever fought girls. Apart from my sisters, which doesn't count. Siblings always fight. It's compulsory, a law of nature; just as it is for mothers to break it up and instinctively side with the littlest one.

When I was small I was physically timid. I would cringe if shouted at. (If I'm honest, I still would, but one of the perks of being a vicar's wife is that people are usually polite to me. It's probably a throwback to feudal times, when priests could curse people and demand tithes.) My family did not go in for shouting and rowing, so I had — and still have — no adequate defences against angry people. This is why it was so unfortunate that I had, as a child, such a knack for calling down anger upon my unprotected head. There was obviously something about me that invited adults and other children to take me down a peg or two. I could never work out what it was. With hindsight, I blame my father. He

11

likes to adopt an absurdly literal approach to language, and he passed this on to us without explaining the dangers. 'Look at all those children running!' a teacher might say, for example. I would look and point out, 'Some of them are walking.' This was purely in the interests of truth, not smart aleckry, and I was always baffled by the reaction I got. What? What? It's true! One teacher nicknamed me 'Catherine Mary, quite contrary'. It's a cruel world. There are adults who cannot find it in themselves to love a cocky child, even when the child is not doing it on purpose.[1]

Trouble at school could be divided into two basic categories. The first was like the weather. It just happened and you had no control over it. You were walking home, it rained, you got wet. Into this category fell the inexplicable rage of teachers and the bullying of older children. If you were in the wrong

---

[1] My older son has more nous than I had, fortunately. In his first week at senior school, his German teacher asked if anyone could count from one to ten. 'In English or German, sir?' my son enquired, shooting his hand up. 'Well, you *could* do it in Japanese if you *prefer*,' sneered the teacher. As it happens, after a year of judo, my son could do this. He had the wit to keep his mouth shut, which I know I wouldn't have.

place at the wrong time, you got bullied. As you went on you learned strategies, like running away, hitting back or telling. Especially telling. We had no truck with that public-school guff about never snitching. If I close my eyes I can still hear the exact intonation of a child in late-1960s Buckinghamshire saying, 'I'm telling of you!'

The other type of trouble was the kind you deserved, or actively sought out. For all the times I was told off *for no reason!*, there were plenty of others when I knew what I was doing. Slapping wet towels on toilet mirrors, for instance. And putting six Hubbly-Bubblies in my mouth in maths and blowing a bubble the size of a netball. It popped and stuck to my glasses. You expect to get into trouble for that kind of thing.

I can't remember how old I was when I began looking for fights at playtime. Around ten, I suspect, just as my hormones were beginning to stir. Yes, I bet it was all hormones. I'd always been a tomboy. Or rather, I'd always wanted to be one. There was nothing that gave me more of a glow than to overhear some other adult saying to my parents, 'She's a real tomboy, isn't she?' Once my father replied ruefully, 'I'm afraid they all are,' which chopped the legs out from under the compliment. I didn't want to be one tomboy among four. I wanted to be the only one. I wanted to be Captain Nancy and fight like a man; not just a naughty girl, but the Naughtiest Girl in the School. I wanted to run away to sea and shin up ropes and sleep in the crow's nest. I wanted never to cry, never to be a sissy, a silly soppy sentimental double-dented disconnected drainpipe, a *girl*.

Worse: second of four girls. People could never remember which of us was which. We were just lumped together as 'the Humphreys girls'. Even my mother used to muddle our names now and then, running through the list randomly till she hit the right one. (Interestingly, though, if we were in trouble, it was always my name that sprang first to my mother's lips: 'Ca-Gra-Ru-Hilary! Stop that!') Maybe that's why I had to be different, better than my sisters. I had to be the one that stood out. I had to win.

Grace was bigger and stronger and older. She couldn't readily be beaten by brute force, so I had to be the one who got the last word. I never, ever, *ever* let her win an argument, so ha ha! (She remembers this even now, oddly enough.) My middle sister, Ruth, recently found a diary she kept when she was a child. One entry from the early seventies reads, 'CATHY IS A FAT FAT PIG AND I HATE HER.' I think this just about sums that era up. We don't compete much these days, except over the obvious things like who paid least for their new boots and whose children have picked up the most parasites. (Nits? Pooh! *Mine* have tapeworms and liver flukes!)

My own diaries from that era contain terse accounts of fights with my deadly enemies — gangs of boys whose names are duly recorded, but about whom I remember nothing. These fights consisted mostly of chasing one another the length and breadth of the school grounds, followed by a bit of barging and scrapping, and — my personal speciality — kicking. I suppose it was a variation of kiss-chase, really, though I would never have believed that at the time. Eurgh! Boys? Hated them.

We fought in school, but occasionally cooperated outside, playing up on the railway lines on hot summer afternoons, with the converging tracks shimmering in the heat, and the smell of spilt diesel on the baking rubble. The overhead cables zizzed with private menace. We threw stones at them. Once I was almost hit by a train. I was relating this, tra la!, one teatime a dozen or so years later, and saw from my mother's ashen face that I'd never got round to mentioning the incident at the time. As far as she was concerned, I'd been round playing at Anne Watson's.

In those days parents let young girls go out for walks, provided they stuck together and came home when they said they would. By the age of ten or eleven, I was allowed to range miles over the Chilterns with a sister or friend, off as far as the top of Ivinghoe Beacon, a hill with a strange chalk scar which everyone knew had been caused by Boadicea's chariot slipping. But under the vague heading of 'going for a walk' also came: playing on the Tarzan rope on the cement works wasteland; bouncing on the conveyor belts in the quarry; marauding round building sites and peeing in the unfinished houses and ripping the polythene in the empty windows with our penknives; sneaking about other people's back gardens at night; and, as we have seen, running across railway bridges when the express from Euston was approaching[1].

Above all, I wanted to be tough. I was determined never to betray a weakness. Not allowing myself to cry absorbed a huge amount of time and energy. It was my one devouring ambition, later joined by an

---

[1] It occurs to me suddenly that I may never have mentioned all this to my mum, either. Sorry.

equally fierce determination never to blush. The trouble was that once I started crying I could never stop. Hours after a savage telling-off from the teacher I would still be hunched over my desk, hiccoughing and blotchy-faced. I must have been a strange combination: timid yet cocky, a tomboy crybaby. There was always a gulf between what I wanted to be, and what I humiliatingly was.

What did I want to be? Oh, I wanted to be tall yet petite, strong, athletic and speak five languages. I wanted to be tanned, with long, long straight jet-black hair that was simultaneously blonde and curly, to set off my intense blue/brown eyes. I wanted to be called Kit or Adrienne. I wanted to be Italian and Welsh. I wanted to be an only child with five older brothers. I wanted to be the admiral's daughter, the only girl on board a ship of men; Maid Marion, the only girl in a forest of men. I wanted to be faster and prettier and cleverer than any other girl in the world.

And I knew I wasn't. In real life I was number two Humphreys girl. I wore blue-framed NHS glasses and talked posh. My plaits were mousy blonde. My fringe was too short, because my mum cut it wonky and kept trying to level it up. I was good at netball and could run fast and jump a long way, but nobody gasped and prophesied, One day this girl will win Olympic gold! More importantly, I couldn't shoot an arrow, or climb hand over hand up ropes; talents I ached for.

But I was bright. I could read. I could imagine. At night, before I fell asleep, my brilliance and strength knew no bounds. Every evening I was the star, finally the only girl in a world of men. I climbed impossibly tall trees, shinned up vertical cliff faces, made death-defying leaps and landed like a cat. I suffered terrible injuries without shedding a tear. I could fight with a sword and a quarterstaff and swim like a fish. I always had a cheeky answer. If at any stage I didn't like the way the action was going, I could reel back and correct it. And if I hit a rich vein of form, I could run mental repeats until I fell asleep.

It wasn't a very big step from daydreaming to writing it all down. I stumbled upon my fiction career as a result of the dreaded five pages of 'Free Writing' we were supposed to produce each week. Every Friday I ended up desperately trying to crank out five poems about cobwebs or harvest. One such Friday, at my wits' end, I sharpened my Black Beauty pencil and wrote: 'It was a mild March day, when the warm winds were blowing.' I had hit upon the idea of writing a long adventure story instead. See how fast those five pages fill up now! Before long I thought of little else.

After *Runnaway* [*sic*] was finished (with the appropriate finding of treasure and trouncing of adults) and a fair copy written up in red ink and illustrated by the author, I embarked on my magnum opus, *Wild Cat's Gang*. This was a boldly escapist tale of a gang of girls who went around beating up their deadly rival gang of boys, finally triumphing over adults and kidnappers. It took me more than a year. I lived and breathed it, worked on it in the evenings, tried to interest my friends in playing selected scenes, took it on holiday, and planned it as I fell asleep each night.

I still have *Wild Cat's Gang*. A year ago, when I was embarking on yet another novel I have now abandoned, I reread my juvenilia, with an eye to cannibalising it. I spent the entire time murmuring, Oh no, oh no! half laughing, half appalled at how hideously revealing it was, how seething with prepubescent sexuality, how transparently it was a showcase for my eleven-year-old self in the role of heroine.

Did I want to be a boy? I would probably have said yes, if I'd been asked back then. It seemed obvious to me that boys had a nicer time of it; but never once in my nocturnal soap operas did I imagine myself male. It was more a question of *not* wanting to be a girl, or not the kind of girl I felt I was expected to be. I didn't want to be ladylike. I wanted to wear trousers and plimsolls. I didn't want to be quiet. I didn't want to wait my turn, or simmer down, or stop showing off and interrupting. What I really wanted was the limelight. And this, I think, is also the true answer to the question I get asked all the time at readings and lectures, *Did you always want to be a writer?* No, I wanted to be the star of the show. I just got better at disguising it.

Perhaps at the heart of it was the dimly perceived injustice of life. At the top of primary school I was bigger and cleverer than almost everyone. But there were some children, who by the low-down and dastardly trick of being male, were stronger and faster. It wasn't my fault, and there was nothing I could do about it. Maybe I chafed against wider injustices I vaguely sensed — the whole world of things men could do that women just didn't back then; the assumption that an education was never wasted on a woman — why, it would leave her all the better equipped to bring up children! The idea that men had careers, while women occasionally had jobs. How we laughed at sex equality and person-hole covers!

The only time my sense of general injustice was properly focused was on the issue of my right to wear trousers to school. I contested it fiercely. As far as I could see, there was *no reason at all* why I couldn't — apart from some cobblers about it 'not being appropriate'. *Why* wasn't it? Because it 'just wasn't'. Because I was a girl. It was so monstrously unfair. Trousers were the symptom, not the cause; but I didn't know it then.

It seemed to me that just because I was a girl, other people — boys — had an advantage. They hadn't earned it; it was simply handed to them. As I looked ahead of me, appalled, I saw that this situation was only going to deteriorate with adolescence. These stupid cheating boys were *all* going to end up bigger and stronger. And what did puberty offer me? Breasts and periods! Thanks a *bunch*. If the adult women around me were anything to judge by, I was going to get steadily worse at all the important things, such as running and climbing trees. For boys the big adventure of life was opening out. For me it was narrowing down.

If it had been possible to halt the process of adolescence by willpower alone, I'd still be eleven years old. We won't call it penis envy. Growing up in a family of daughters, I seldom glimpsed a penis, and when I did, it certainly didn't make me feel like a man manqué. Freud was wrong about that, surely. A penis looked more like an addition to me, a puzzling and slightly shocking growth of some kind. Something that my friends and I would snort and giggle over and recite rude rhymes about: *My friend Billy had a ten-foot willy, / He showed it to the girl next door.*

Life is tough for the ultra-competitive bad loser. That was the awful thing about growing up. I could see the odds would be stacked more and more against me. Prudence warned that I wasn't going to be able to chase boys and kick them for very much longer. If I caught them at all, they would only kick me back twice as hard. I would just have to find other ways of winning.

When I look back to the last year before my body betrayed me, I can still sometimes recapture that feeling of aching, yearning potency, of being able to run so fast I could nearly, oh, nearly-*nearly* get airborne. In another moment I was going to learn the trick of it. I was on the very brink of being invincible. Writing fiction felt the same — still does, in fact, when it's going well.

It was in my year of world domination, alongside all that fierce writing and kick-chase and netball, that I discovered judo.

* ★ *

Nowadays I live in the Black Country, but I grew up in what should have been called the White Country. The four, and later on, five chimneys of Tunnel Cement dominated the skyline of my childhood, snowing white dust all over the neighbourhood. It was like growing up in a grubby Narnia. The trees and hedges, grass verges, roads and rooftops, all had a layer of dust that the rain had hardened to a concrete finish. My father used to clean our car with steel wool. If I looked out across the chalky, flinty wheat fields at the front of our house I could see the low line of the Chilterns in the distance. At the back of the house, half a mile off, was the factory. It clashed and groaned and jangled all day and night. Red cement lorries came and went the whole time.

Tunnel Cement was the major local employer. This meant that when someone opened a judo club in the canteen, everyone at our school knew about it. It was instantly popular. My friend Angela, whose dad worked at Tunnel, used to go with her brothers. Before long my older sister and I were going too, walking with the others across the recreation ground on Friday evenings with our judogis slung across our shoulders by the belt.

The club was run by someone we called sensei. I can't remember what his real name was. He must have been in his late thirties; *old* by our standards, at any rate. He was dark-haired and swarthy and had a northern accent. Best of all, he was *a black belt*. He told us that he took up judo in order to be able to beat up someone he hated. But by the time he was a blue belt, he no longer needed to. He had learned self-discipline. He could have thrashed his enemy next time they met. Instead he walked away from the fight. The nobility of this impressed me deeply.

It was a pretty rough-and-tumble club. In the days before child protection and lawsuits there was no fannying about with health and safety issues. We used to do diving breakfalls over a line of curled-up clubmates, like motorbike stunt drivers jumping double-decker buses. If anyone got hurt they were sprayed liberally with Ralgex painkiller and expected to get on with it.

I showed early promise. At last, a place where I could duff people up and not get told off! Where aggression was praised, not rebuked as unladylike! Where trousers were compulsory! Once I threw my sister Grace with a technique called *morote-seoi-nage*, a big killer throw that wallops your opponent over your shoulder onto the mat. I collapsed under her weight and ended up throwing from my knees. 'That,' said sensei, 'is the best throw I have ever seen by a junior.' At one stage, he took Grace and me to one side and told us solemnly, 'You two could be black belts if you carry on. You're good enough.'[1] So to start with, I loved it, though I did spend a lot of time off the mat watching. Nobody worried about litigation in the early seventies, but everyone was terrified of veruccas. I developed a fine crop and was therefore not allowed to swim or do judo until my father had burnt them off with formaldehyde.

After about two years the club shut down. I think sensei had a row with the Tunnel Cement people and took his mats home. This kind of thing is common in martial arts, I've since come to realise. Testosterone, probably. I should have been devastated, but secretly I was glad. It gave me an honourable reason for giving up. The problem, in the end, was a combination of sensei and the onset of adolescence. He liked to tease me, and twelve is a sensitive

---

[1] I asked my sister recently if she remembered this. She laughed and said, 'Yeah, but I didn't believe him.' I did.

age. He used to say how vicious I was, what a temper I had. 'Ooh, she'll murder someone one day, you watch!' It was probably my determination and the faces I pulled. I couldn't wear my glasses on the mat. Screwing your eyes up improves your vision slightly if you are short-sighted, but it does make you look mean. The baiting meant that judo stopped being fun, so I was relieved to be giving it up.

I didn't entirely give up thinking about it, though. The tall dark handsome hero of *Wild Cat's Gang* (an early prototype for later heroes I very much fear), was a judo black belt. I still remembered some of the techniques and their names, but as I grew older the tomboy gradually mutated into a grammar-school swot. My competitive energies were mostly rechannelled into beating Mary Green in chemistry tests.

My body mutated too. I belatedly worked out that there were compensations for growing breasts. Maybe you couldn't run any more without folding your arms across your chest, but breasts gave you power of a different sort. Aha! No need to kick boys when all you had to do to gain the upper hand was wear a tight T-shirt. From then on, the only inter-gender skirmishing I went in for was verbal. I was probably slow to grasp that boys were keener on breasts than rapier wit, and that they were unlikely to play Benedick to my Beatrice when there were other less bracing girls around in lower-cut dresses.

In the end, my *judogi* went to a jumble sale, just like my ballet leotard had done a few years before. Judo was filed under the heading of childhood crazes, along with things like gymnastics, French knitting, horse riding and Plasticraft. Something you did for a while, then dropped.

★ ★ ★

Back at the very beginnings of martial arts, white was the only colour of belt. You acquired a black belt by dint of practising for so long that your belt became blackened by age, dirt, sweat and the blood of a thousand opponents. This is told to us as a means of encouragement. See? It is only a matter of time before you too have a black belt. Keep going! The idea is still enshrined in the progression of colours the successful player passes through. They grow increasingly dark: from yellow, through orange, green, blue, brown, until finally, of course, we reach black.

But white belt is where it all begins.

What is Judo?

It is worth clearing up a common misconception at the outset. 'Martial arts? Well, they're all basically the same, aren't they?' goes the opinion of your armchair expert. 'I mean, you all wear those white pyjamas, don't you?' This is about as clever as saying all religions are the same because the men in charge all wear long frocks.

When I tell people I do judo, most of them instantly adopt what they take to be a martial arts pose, then flail about with their arms and legs. They will probably make pseudo-oriental yipping noises as well — 'Eeeee-*hoh*! Judo chop!' — based on distant memories of Bruce Lee movies. 'There's no striking or kicking in judo,' I say coldly. 'Oh,' they say, straightening back up. 'What do you do in judo, then?' I explain that it is basically wrestling. If they say, 'That sounds boring,' I toss them on their head and say, 'Yes, it is a bit.'

Depressingly for us judo enthusiasts, most people in the UK think karate when they think martial arts. If you go into a big bookshop and browse in the sport section, you will usually find a dozen karate books for every book on judo. Karate is cool. I know this for a fact, because I asked my (then) thirteen-year-old son. It is cool because you learn how to kill people and chop breeze blocks in half.

Why bother with a fighting sport that renounces these glamorous and handy life skills? I try telling him that you aren't actually supposed to land punches or kicks when you learn karate, it's *meant* to be non-contact. Whereas judo . . . He cuts me off with that masterly teen summing-up of any discussion: 'Whatever.'

The main reason judo isn't cool is because his mum does it. This is entirely reasonable, and I accept it. Judo would, however, instantly become cool if I got a black belt, which is quite an incentive. Think: if I got a black belt, I could wear my embarrassing Donny Osmond tribute hat in public *and still be cool!*

For those of you seeking an authoritative account of the origins of judo, let me point you without delay in the direction of *Kodokan Judo*, by the master himself, Jigoro Kano. It was Professor Kano who founded judo in Japan back in 1882. In his book you will find the history, ethos and all the techniques described with suitable gravitas and uninterrupted by silly references to Donny Osmond. But for those of you who prefer a spoonful of sugar with your medicine — or better still, half a pound of Belgian chocolates — stay with me.

Jigoro Kano was born in Mikage on 28 October 1860. Please don't picture him as a mindless killing machine. He was a fine academic, graduating in literature, politics and political economy from Tokyo Imperial University in 1881, and becoming a professor, and later vice principal, at Gakushuin. His picture still hangs in many dojos, and players practise under his shrewd, slightly sorrowful gaze, and bow in his direction at the beginning and end of their sessions as a mark of respect.

By his own account, Kano spent many years in his youth studying ju-jitsu under a variety of masters. Kano observed that techniques changed from teacher to teacher. Confused by this, he set himself the task of seeking out the principle underlying all the strikes and throws he'd learned. The principle was, he concluded, to make the most efficient use of energy, both mental and physical. 'Maximum efficiency' became his touchstone, and he rejected any methods of attack and defence that were not in harmony with it. What he ended up with was a code of formalised techniques in four main categories: throws, pindowns, armlocks and strangles. To this he gave the name 'judo', so as to distinguish it from the earlier term, 'ju-jitsu'. Ju-jitsu (also spelt ju-jutsu) is probably best regarded as judo's psychotic older relative — an observation based on the ju-jitsu players I've met, rather than any formal study.

Minimum effort and maximum efficiency. Is there anyone who doesn't warm to this? It is a fine principle, one we unconsciously apply all the time in our daily lives. The principle of maximum efficiency tells us to put the biscuit tin on the kitchen table in front of us, not at the bottom of the garden. It instructs us that by using the minimum effort — maybe a small bribe or threat — we can persuade our children to fetch us another beer, rather than expending valuable energy getting it ourselves and possibly missing a crucial penalty.

It is this principle of getting someone else to do the hard work for you that underlies good judo. I say 'good' judo, because I find maximum efficiency a strangely elusive concept when I am on the mat fighting. Maximum efficiency, maximum efficiency! I mutter to myself as I bow to my opponent, but within seconds it has fled my mind. I fight as though I'm trying to wrestle a moose, or an industrial washing machine.[1] Once in a

---

[1] I told my coach Keith this, and he said, 'You know what, you *could* move a really heavy washing machine, if you got it rocking.' See? A good judo player understands these things.

while I get a glimpse of how sweet it could be. I go for a foot sweep without really thinking about it, and the timing is spot on. I look down in astonishment and there is my opponent flat on her back. Wow, I must try that again! I think. I try it again. It doesn't work. In a few minutes I'm back to grunting.

The heart of it is giving way. Kano explains that this is what the 'ju' in both judo and ju-jitsu means: 'gentleness' or 'giving way'. If your martial model is the drunken English street brawl, then this feels perverse. Gentleness? I came here for a fight! But as you watch and train with more experienced judo players, you soon grasp that giving way doesn't mean backing down. Far from it. Gentleness is a lethal strategy. *Kodokan Judo* offers several nice cameos to illustrate the principle, and it's worth quoting the first one in full, as Kano, with his customary efficiency, expresses it far more elegantly than I ever could:

Let us say a man is standing before me whose strength is ten, and that my own strength is but seven. If he pushes me as hard as he can, I am sure to be pushed back or knocked down, even if I resist with all my might. This is opposing strength with strength. But if instead of opposing him I give way to the extent he has pushed, withdrawing my body and maintaining my balance, my opponent will lose his balance. Weakened by his awkward position, he will be unable to use all his strength. It will have fallen to three. Because I retain my balance, my strength remains at seven. Now I am stronger than my opponent and can defeat him by using only half my strength, keeping the other half available for some other purpose. Even if you are stronger than your opponent, it is better first to give way. By doing so you conserve energy while exhausting your opponent.

When I was a horrid little girl at primary school, I sometimes used to trip other children up. Even now if someone is hurrying past me, I occasionally get an urge to stick out a foot. If I yielded to the temptation, my victim's own momentum would cause her or him to crash headlong. I would — with maximum efficiency and conservation of energy, tada! — have brought about the fall by a single economical movement. Well, obviously we vicars' wives don't go around tripping people up, but you see what I'm driving at. It's the same in rugby: a small wing can bring down a great lumbering rhino of a forward by a brave tackle round the ankles.

Balance is the key: keeping your own balance and breaking your opponent's. You learn this rapidly if you don't want to be thrown. But because you are always fighting people who are mastering the same skills, you might not realise how effective your techniques are becoming. I'd been doing judo for about six months when Gary at church asked me what I'd learned. You must never, NEVER use judo techniques outside the dojo. Professor Kano is quite stern about this, so I totally deny that I kind of half showed Gary a couple of techniques. Without actually throwing him, of course. Gary is a roofer, about my height, but built like Rambo. All I did was take hold of him and tug a bit one way, and push a bit the other, possibly using my sneaky tripping-up foot at the same time, and I was amazed to see his arms wind-milling as he struggled to keep his balance. Although, as I said, I totally deny the whole incident. And anyway, he wasn't hurt. Not even his pride was hurt, because 'he let me do it'. The phrase 'I let you do it' (with its companion 'I could have got out of it if I'd wanted to') is one that all women judo players quickly become familiar with.

So that's judo for you. No chopping, no kicking. Maximum efficiency. Give way, keep your balance. Sorted. And now on to that all-important question: what am I going to wear?

Your First Judogi

When you buy your very first judo suit, it comes with a white belt. A judo kit, or *judogi*, as it is properly known, traditionally consists of a thick white cotton jacket, tied with a belt, and a pair of baggy white drawstring trousers in somewhat thinner material, reinforced at the knees. Your suit comes flat-packed, looking bafflingly like an IKEA canvas sofa cover. When you take it out of its plastic bag, you will be amazed at how stiff the jacket is. You break your nails on it and wonder if putting it on and managing to bend your arms is all part of the training. Because of the high level of hands-on scragging involved, judo jackets need to be far thicker and tougher than their karate or aikido equivalents. (The same might be said for the players.)

The jacket, or *gi*, is generously cut and designed to fit a fridge. At first it will be far too big, but that's OK. Give it a hot wash and it will shrink to fit you — if you happen to be fridge-shaped. I have come up against players who are. I am not fridge-shaped myself, unless you are visualising a tallish and (I like

35

to imagine) slimline model. The trousers shrink as well and because I'm quite tall this means that mine are always an attractive mid-shin Bay City Roller length. This is no bad thing in judo terms. The smaller and tighter your suit, the less there is for your opponent to grab hold of.

The first thing to put on is your trousers. (We will discuss underwear later.) Here's an important piece of mental preparation vis-à-vis judo trousers: your bum *will* look big in them. There is way too much material, and when you tighten the drawstring, it all bunches up round the waist. We all know that this is not a good look, but just get over it. Judo trousers are completely egalitarian: *everyone's* bum looks big in them. Another consoling thought is that a low centre of gravity is a real advantage on the mat, as it makes you much harder to throw. So cheer up — the bigger the better! Where else can that be said? And anyway, the jacket is long enough to cover everything.

To put your new jacket on, first bend and pummel it a little so that you can manipulate your arms through the sleeves. Cross the right side tightly over your chest — imagine wrapping a heavy-duty cardboard dressing gown round you — then cross the left side over the top of that. At first this will feel awkward to women, as our clothes generally do up the opposite way, but there are two reasons why it has to be like this. Firstly, a conventional grip involves your opponent taking a right-handed grasp of your left lapel. If you have your jacket done up the girl way, your whole suit will soon be in total disarray. In a contest the ref will stop the fight and give the signal for you to readjust your *judogi*. The second reason is that left-over-right is the way Professor Kano told us it should be done. Respect, you see. We bow to his way of doing things. I'm told that right-over-left is reserved for corpses being laid out in Japan, and therefore deeply offensive in the living. Not to say inauspicious on the judo mat.

Now we come to the belt. This will be similar to tying a metal curtain rod round your middle, so the thing to do when you get home is put the belt round the banister and twist it as tight as you can, first one way, then the other, and run it through the washing machine a couple of hundred times to soften it up. Alternatively, get a clubmate to hold the other end and both of you twist in opposite directions. Once it is sufficiently pliable, place the middle of the belt on the centre front of your waist. Pass both ends behind your back and bring them round to the front again. Tie it in a knot at the centre front, making sure that one end has been tucked under the whole belt, to anchor it. Tie another knot, then pull both ends sharply to tighten.

Don't worry if you got lost halfway through that description, despite miming it out to yourself as you went along. This is the very first lesson in judo, and probably in any sport — you have to be *shown* what to do, not just told. In any case, I'm only explaining how I, personally, tie my belt. Every so often some sneering higher-grade bloke flicks at it contemptuously and says, 'What's *this*? Can't you tie a belt yet?' To which I reply, 'Oh, shut up.' (Under my breath.)

So there you are, all kitted out in your brand-new *judogi*. Women players are allowed to wear a plain white T-shirt under their jacket. I mention that in case anyone was getting worried — or, indeed, excited. Your feet ought to be bare in your trainers/flip-flops/sandals as you must go barefoot on the mat at all times. Don't walk around without shoes off the mat, though, as this is bad form. By now you will have stripped off your watch and all your jewellery, including your plain wedding ring if you have one. I used to think impatiently, How on earth could you injure anything with a wedding ring? That was before I jumped down the last few steps from our loft one day with my ring hooked on the top of the ladder. Aha! *That's* how. Happily, the ring gave way before the finger did, which I interpret as God's method of rewarding me for being a low-maintenance bride all those years before and only wanting a cheap ring. If you have medical friends, why not freak yourself out by asking them what 'de-gloving' means in this context?

On that grisly note, I believe I have now delivered you, safely and properly attired, to the edge of the mat, ready to learn your first throw. Abandon your shoes, bow (if you are strong enough to bend in your new kit) and take your first step out into the big bad world of judo.

Your First Throw

The first throw you will learn as a senior player in a British Judo Association (BJA) affiliated club is *o-goshi*,[1] or 'major hip throw'. Here's how to do it:

---

[1] As you probably spotted, this Japanese term provides an opportunity for humour. Beginners are sometimes told that the technique gets its name because 'Oh gosh!' is what you say while you are being thrown. Not true, of course, but as far as I know there isn't a throw called *o-shiti*.

Draw your partner onto his toes as you step in. Move the right foot forward and diagonally across to your left placing it just in front of your opponent's right foot. Pivoting on this, swing your left foot back and round so both your heels are apart with your feet comfortably placed. Your knees should be well bent with your belt lower than his. At your first step drive your right arm between his left arm and body and, placing the palm flat against his back, lock him to you. The throw is completed by straightening your legs and bending forward and twisting slightly to your left. Swing him over your hips and down onto the mat.

That should be sufficient to prove that there's no such thing as distance learning in judo. Even if your description is accompanied by illustrations, you will still struggle.[1] You have to be shown — safely, by an accredited coach (who you may address respectfully as 'sensei') — what to do, then you have to have a go for yourself. Standing there like a lemon trying to

_____

[1] The BJA syllabus, from which the above extract is taken, contains illustrations. These occasionally remind me of a dangerously ambitious *Joy of Sex*, only without the beards.

get your head round a new technique is a waste of time. You have to get your body round it. The knowledge has to get past the intellect and into your muscle memory. This is hard for people like me who have spent far too long in libraries and prefer to gain their new information from books.

Here's another thing, a slightly scary thing: you have to try before you really know what you are doing, because it is only through doing it that you will find out. I say scary, because deep down I nurse a secret and lifelong aim never to make a fool of myself. Yes, I know — a ridiculous ambition. What's my problem? We are all foolish people who do foolish things from time to time. Wouldn't it be nice to have the humility/security/sense of worth — or whatever it is — not to mind? Because if you genuinely don't mind making a fool of yourself, you never truly will. I'll know I'm a proper grown-up when I achieve this state. The acid test will be dispensing with the safety net of self-deprecating irony. I'm talking about that knee-jerk impulse to get a pre-emptive laugh in at yourself first. Oddly enough, judo offers a safe place to try out this kind of thing. If you find the right club, that is. I'm sure there are nasty, unsupportive dojos out there, but mine isn't like that. I will get my leg pulled, but I know that my coaches and clubmates aren't going to line up like a row of Nelsons from *The Simpsons* and jeer 'Ha ha!' every time I make a mistake.

It would be a great shame, in my forties, still to be held back by the ghosts from childhood snickering at me. Perhaps if I hadn't taken that *Ha ha!* so seriously as a child, I'd be a better person now. I might not have ended up as a writer, though. Many writers — I'm tempted to say all — are afflicted by a pathetic but quite genuine need for universal love and approval. This is heartbreaking, really, since the very act of getting published means you have stuck your head above the parapet with a target on your face, saying 'Arrows here, please'. Every writer I have ever met can quote at length, verbatim, their worst reviews, years after anything positive has faded from their memory (withered by the thought *If I'm that good, how come I didn't get shortlisted for anything?*).

The system would work much better if along with the gift of writing came a complementary rhino hide, a psychological firewall-cum-anti-virus package to protect the delicate ego. Yes, I *know* this kind of whingeing is extremely irritating. If you dish it out, people say, you should be able to take it. But, as Michael Bywater once brilliantly observed in his column in the *Independent*, dishing it out and taking it are widely different talents. It is completely unreasonable to expect them to be combined in one individual.

Judo is not just about physical fitness. Yes, you will reach the point where you have been thrown so many times it no longer really bothers you. But there will also come a time when you stop worrying about looking like a prat, when your fear of failure is no longer a barrier to having a go at something. After a few months on the mat, even the most fragile ego toughens up a bit, too.

Get over yourself. Get a grip. Literally. Kit on, shoes off, tie your hair back and remember — no crying, even if your mascara is totally waterproof.

You're in the dojo now, soldier.

Diary

12 February 2005

The night before the Big Day. I'd coped all right until I went to the Oak Park club this afternoon, when all the talk was about dirty tactics, which brings the raw horror flooding back. It's over two years since I last went to a grading. I need to win two fights to get my 1st kyu, my top brown belt. What I *had* been feeling was pretty upbeat and cheerful, a state of mind achieved mostly by resolutely not thinking about it at all. If I sit and *visualise*, the way you're supposed to, my pulse starts racing and my heart pounding. This is particularly bad news if I am in bed trying to sleep.

Whether my strategy of denial will work through tonight, I don't know. I'll try and get everything ready before I go to bed, so that I can't lie there making to-do lists. Iron kit. Pack bag. I will pray for calm. I prayed this morning for Everyone Else Attending the Grading. (A Trojan horse prayer for my own selfish petition for success. It fools God every time.) The tricky thing about praying for sporting success is that it can only come at the expense of others. I prayed that there would be no serious injuries, no broken bones tomorrow. When I stop to think, I have never actually had a really dreadful time at a grading. I've always graded up, and I've never been badly hurt, and apart from that strangling incident, I've never injured anyone.

I seek consolation in the old thought that this time tomorrow it will all be over. My older son was trying to brace me up this morning. 'You've got nothing to lose,' he pointed out. 'My pride? My dignity?' I suggested. 'You lost *them* ages ago,' he replied. The only question is: Do I want a black belt enough to put myself through this ordeal? The answer is still: Yes. Yes I do. Only please let everyone be nice to me. Don't let it be horrible.

Hymn of the Week is John Bunyan's 'He who would Valiant be'. I've doctored the words to make them inclusive of me, a mere woman pilgrim. 'No foe shall stay my might, / I'll with a giant fight — [*hope not, but I will be with the big girls because, frankly, I am one*] — But I'll make good my right to be a pilgrim!' I like the lusty Nonconformist 'stuff you' nature of these words. 'Then fancies flee away, I'll fear not what men say! I'll labour night and day to be a pilgrim.' Poor old Bunyan was locked up when he wrote them, I think.

14 February 2005

YESS!!! Won both my contests yesterday and am now 1st kyu! I was lucky on the day. Not a big turnout, possibly because it was half-term. There were hardly any kyu-grade women, and only one other brown belt and a single blue belt, a clubmate Natalie from Wolverhampton Youth Judo Club, who I fight every week. But that's the way it goes. Luck is all part of it.

How nice it all is, looking back. Slept reasonably well on Saturday night. My alarm went off at 6.45 a.m. Ate my oat bran porridge with raspberries as usual; slow-burn carbs being what you need, according to Keith, my coach. Palestrina was playing plangently on the kitchen CD player. *Miserere, miserere nobis*. Had a shower and washed my hair and waxed it up into my scary-woman style, as if electrified and still fizzing with energy. Put the meat in the oven, so it would be ready for when Pete and the boys got in from church. Went to the loo a couple of hundred times. Took my battery of dietary supplements.

Packed bag with lucky New Zealand judo kit, lucky New Zealand white T-shirt, plus shorts (in case lucky trousers split), spare trousers (ditto); micropore and plasters to tape up finger so I don't bleed on people; banana and flapjack (more slow-burn carbs in case it goes on all day), two half-litre bottles of water; licence, money, lipsalve, spare contact lenses in case I lose one, spare glasses in case of eye injury, mobile to ring home with results/beg for lift; hat and gloves in case I end up walking.

Pete drove me to the new judo centre. Walked bravely in and caught sight of Keith by one of the weigh stations, which made me feel a bit better. Got weighed. Seventy-two kilos, wow, an unbelievable nine stone three! Unbelievable, in the sense that it's *actually* about eleven and a half stone, but most people don't know that, fortunately. Besides, it's all chest and muscle. And brains. Brains are heavy.

Went to pay, and caught the eye of a nice Italian woman, who proclaimed herself scared. I smiled and said that I thought everyone was. She turned to her coach and said, 'She seems nice. Can I fight her?' It's so important to me to spread a bit of niceness around. These occasions need humanising and making personal. I'm a living person, a mother, I make cakes and stuff! Can't we be friends?

The new judo centre is amazing. Blond wood and brushed-chrome door handles, Costa coffee. The arena has a square of four full-sized matted areas, each individual mat being the new small square kind, not the big old rectangles we have to heave about at Oak Park. As you enter, there is banked seating to your right, so you don't get spectators crowding round all sides baying with bloodlust like madmen at a cockfight. They still shout, of course, just from a greater distance.

Debbie and Heather, my other coaches, had arrived and bagged a couple of rows of seats at the back nearest the entrance. I was on the mat furthest from them as it happened, but that was no real problem given the acoustics. Debbie, in particular, knows how to project her voice and foghorn from the diaphragm. 'COME ON, CATH!' In fact, she came down and stood as near to the mat edge as possible to give us moral support, but I could hear Heather and Jo (Heather's twin who no longer does judo after a bad injury) and Debbie's mum, Dee, bawling clear across the arena. This is unusual. Normally the adrenalin renders me deaf.

Sharon arrived, looking even more scared than I felt. We went to get changed together. Company makes it more bearable. In the changing rooms a mother was plaiting her teenage daughter's hair. Sharon and I wondered aloud why we were putting ourselves through this, we were too old. The mother said, 'Well, I got my black belt last year and I'm forty-three!' This is what we want to hear. She also added, less helpfully, that she was *never* going to go to another grading.

Back into the echoing arena, which was filling up. The usual hanging around before we were called on to the mat. This is when the psyching out takes place. Many of the players wander around without their belts on, *gi* flapping open, so as not to betray to the opposition what grade they are. Look mean, counselled Debbie. They're sizing you up. Look mean, as opposed to petrified. Right.

Scary psycho teenagers with GBR in foot-high letters on their backs jogging round the perimeter of all four mats, or throwing imaginary opponents with incredibly fast drop-knee *seoi-nages*. The girl who broke Jo's arm last November was among them. I decided not to join in. It would probably wear me out. So would shadow-throwing. Besides, it would betray my favourite techniques to those sizing me up. Plus I'd feel stupid.

Big blokes were prowling around, hoodies under their jackets, all unshaven, which is the etiquette. A sort of testosterone signaller, I suppose, pretending that three days' worth of beard has sprouted overnight. It can be useful in groundwork. You can stubble-burn your opponent into submission. I certainly didn't shave my legs.

Lots of stretching out and warming up going on all round the mat edges. One young woman was being drilled on the proper bowing-on routine on the edge of the 1st kyu mat, the mat I'd be on next time if I won today. Debbie curled her lip. If she doesn't know how to bow on properly by now, she shouldn't be going for her dan grade. This is the worst bit of the many very, very bad bits about gradings. The waiting, the firing-squad-at-dawn waiting.

But today, mercifully, it was over quickly. The 'ladies' kyu grades were called straight away onto the far mat nearest the seating. We lined up in grade order, me as the highest grade. Aha, I thought, and began to feel stealthily confident. The other brown belt was also a vet, possibly older than me, certainly smaller, and not looking particularly happy. She told me she 'didn't like the shouting'. I knew that Debbie was nice and handy for some point-blank foghorning, so I thought, *Oh dear*, in a hypocritical way.

It was pretty clear to me by then that I was going to get two fights, one with Nat, and one with the woman who hated shouting. I knew I had a good chance of winning both, unless my sense of fair play undermined me, as it has done on several occasions before when I've been up against a clubmate I normally beat.

Sharon was beaten and wanted to withdraw. Debbie talked her out of it. Nat beat the brown belt. I'm ashamed to say I shouted. Several more bouts, including the nice Italian woman. The ref (in his blazer and grey slacks and black socks) seemed to be allowing an unusually long time for groundwork, which is good for me. I prefer being on the ground partly because my strangles and armlocks are good, mostly because you can't get thrown. Keith was at the desk adjudicating.

Nat and I were called out. I tied on the red belt while she put on the white. We grinned at one another and shrugged and said we'd both do our best, what else could we say? I tried to focus. Don't be soft just because you are a higher grade, taller, stronger, old enough to be her mother, normally beat her and are at least two stone heavier, I told myself. The little tinker came at me like a tiger and bloody nearly won, so I didn't feel too bad when I took her down and got a *waza-ari* score (7 points) and then just as the four minutes was nearly up, an *ippon* (10 points) off a scrambled *o-soto-gari*. Anyway, she'd already beaten the other brown belt, which meant she was going to grade up whatever. I needed it more. OK? It was the closest to fun a grading has ever been, partly because of the roars of 'Come on, both of yer!' from our even-handed clubmates.

Sharon was up again and almost threw her opponent, but landed on her face. Medics came on to pinch her nose for her. They went off, and the fight continued. So many near throws with me and Deb shouting 'YESS — oh!' and doing that despairing hands-clasped-round-the-back-of-the-neck routine so popular with Newcastle fans. At the very last moment Sharon threw her opponent and punched the air. She went on to win her next contest as well, and looked like a right bruiser afterwards with bashed nose and swollen lips.

I got called up for my second bout — against the other brown belt. 'GOOD LUCK!' I bellowed in her face. Of course I didn't. Deb took me by the shoulders and looked me in the eye. 'You can win this.' She went on to say a lot more, but I'm afraid my mind was totally blank. I vaguely remember her saying. 'You're strong. You don't think it, but you are.' With me nodding earnestly throughout. I stepped on to the mat as relaxed as I am ever going to be. But in my mind, unbelievably, was the thought, *I'm going to win this*.

I did. I can't reconstruct much of it now, apart from the fact that she was stiff-arming me, so I *tomoenage-ed* her. E-ver-so-slow-ly. And got a *waza-ari*. I'm amazed I had the nerve to try it at all, even in slow motion. It's a throw I never use. My other memory is of wondering why the hell she wasn't getting penalised for passivity, as I wasn't aware of any attacks.

And that was that. We lined up again and

bowed off, and I went to get changed. As I was making my way back to where Keith and Debbie and the rest of my clubmates were gathered for post-mortems, I was intercepted by the woman official for our mat, who handed back my licence with the words, 'Congratulations, see you at the dan grading next time.'

I'm still grinning. I don't mind the piss-taking from Keith about the slow-mo *tomoe-nage*, I don't mind the aching shoulders and neck. *I'm going for my dan grade.*

Walked to St Paul's in the cold February sunshine, munching flapjack and banana and swigging from my water bottle as I went. Arrived back at church in time for the Eucharistic Prayer, giving Pete the thumbs up as he stood behind the communion table presiding. The last hymn was 'What a Friend We Have in Jesus', one of my favourites. Went home for lunch and made some fairy cakes in the afternoon to restore the natural equilibrium of the universe. I am a nice person. I kick ass, but I bake fairy cakes as well.

2

Yellow Belt

Run the straight race through God's good
   grace,
Lift up thine eyes, and seek his face;
Life with its way before us lies,
Christ is the path, and Christ the prize.

Verse 2, Hymn 54, 'Fight the Good Fight'
                in *With Cheerful Voice:*
                     Hymns for Children

Running the Straight Race

Running is a useful life metaphor. It is
accessible — most of us know what it's like to
run, even if we aren't in the habit of doing it
much any more. It is also broad, encompass-
ing everything from the unwelcome trot for a
bus to full-blown fell running. In the hymn,
'straight' implies that life is a 100-metre race,
which makes me suspect the word is only
there to make the line scan — unless,

perhaps, the hymn writer was trying to inspire a manly, future-governors-of-the-Empire decency in the congregation. The Bible verse that lies behind it reads 'Let us run with perseverance the race that is set before us'. Perseverance suggests long distances over tough terrain, struggling through mud and brambles, uphill with the rain in your face. Life as cross-country, not sprint.

My running career has been patchy. As a school-girl I was pretty fast. On sports day I could count on being in the top few places in the 100 or 200 metres. My competitiveness meant that I was bad at longer races. I couldn't bear being left behind, so I killed myself trying to keep up with the distance runners, only to cross the line last with the slow girls and promptly throw up. At the age of fourteen I visualised life, ideally, as a swift dash: modest effort allied to natural brilliance, followed by a well-deserved lap of honour. Slogging, whether on the playing field or in the classroom, seemed to me a mug's game.

It wasn't until my early twenties that I discovered an appetite for longer distances. I was at Durham University, researching for an MA in the theology department and hating it. A couple of times a week I would escape from my books and card-file index and run for six, seven, occasionally ten miles around the city. My mental image of life's race expanded. I could grind out those tedious miles after all. I didn't give up on long hills. Although I persevered with the research for six more years, oddly enough, I dropped the running.

Something strange happens to many people at forty. 'Here I am,' goes the thought, 'flabby, middle-aged, children growing up, ambitions not realised — what's the point of me? I know, I'll run a marathon.' This may sound like a non sequitur, but at some level it makes profound sense. For the lifelong non-runner doing a marathon is a huge challenge. It requires courage and grit and persistence, to say nothing of a complete physical transformation. But one of the attractions is that while it's tough, it's not completely unthinkable. Managing to run 26 miles and 385 yards says a lot about the middle-aged you: 'Against the odds I have turned my life around! I have become something I'd given up hope of being! I have overcome! (As well as raising an impressive amount of money for the charity of my choice!)' To the non-running observer, of course, it may say something completely different, like 'You're bonkers!' But one way or another, running a marathon helps bridge the ever widening gap between your inner and outer self.

A few summers ago I stood on a bridge in Durham in the sunshine, admiring the cathedral and gazing down at the river as I'd done many times when I was a student. My hands were resting on the parapet. I stared at them and found myself thinking, 'There is probably not a single cell in my body that is the same as when I stood here twenty-two years ago. In what sense am I still the same person?' Well, I thought, even though my body has been completely replaced, block by block, the same mind is still inhabiting it. Surely? But I found, looking back at my twenty-year-old self, that I didn't even feel as if I had the same mind. I puzzle now and then about whether my body is me, what the relationship is between brain and mind, who I really am. Then I decide that trying to understand the mystery of human consciousness is like trying to pick yourself up in a bucket. It can't be done.

I saw a survey a while back on 'What Women Want'. We want two things, it turns out: world peace and thinner thighs. (In that order, because nobody wants to look shallow.) We live in an image-obsessed society. We are prone to think of our bodies as the house our personality lives in. Naturally we are ambitious. Who wants a pigsty when they can live in a luxury penthouse or, better still, a wisteria-covered eight-bedroom former rectory in a picturesque village? But however blessed we are by our niche in the property market, it gradually dawns on us that our home is beginning to look a bit run-down. It sags and creaks as the years take their toll. We undertake an urgent schedule of repair work: diets, keepfit, Botox, colonic irrigation, liposuction. No more horizontal stripes! Suck that belly in! Leave that shirt hanging out! Switch to grape products! But in the end we discover we are living in one of those hotels on the Yorkshire coast. You wake up one morning and half of it has fallen into the sea. The rest's going to follow and there ain't nothing you can do about it.

This imagery feels a bit unaffectionate. After all, your body is your best and oldest mate, your ally. You've been through a lot together. You're on the same team. I try to think this, but occasionally I'm a bit unkind to my old pal, in the manner of a sadistic PE mistress. GET UP — YOU'RE NOT HURT! FASTER! COME ALONG! LAST ONE BACK HAS TO DO IT AGAIN! I wouldn't treat anyone else this harshly, making them go out running when they really aren't well and never letting them eat Penguin bars.

I suspect that body image shifts as societies change. When Britain was a more heavily industrialised society, we needed manual workers. Bodies were useful for manufacturing things, for physical labour. What are bodies for in a consumer society? For consuming things, obviously: food, drink, sex, entertainment, fashion, technology. What is this body of mine *for*, now the mind does most of the work, sitting at a desk in front of a computer, or slumped on the sofa in front of the TV?

Here are some possible answers: the body gets me from A to B (Body as vehicle). The body is what makes the mind possible (Body as computer hardware). The body is what I enjoy myself with (Body as party venue). The body is how I project my image (Body as advert).

Not forgetting Body as biological destiny. About fifteen years ago my GP's surgery was handing out a questionnaire to its patients as part of some research into eating disorders. It asked how much I weighed and how I felt about my body. The answer to the first question was 'About ten tons'; to the second, 'FANTASTIC!' This was because I'd just had my first baby. Addled by happy hormones, I was far too impressed by my achievement to bother about flab. My body had done what it was designed to do.

This sense of biological fulfilment comes to

most women only a handful of times, and to others not at all. So what's the female body for the rest of the time? And what about men, come to think of it, now Sainsbury's has replaced mammoth-hunting, and the old-style Viking rape-and-pillage approach to life is frowned upon?

Looking back, I can see that taking up judo was a marathon substitute: Here's something my body *can* do. I didn't think about it consciously, but judo must have been a way of answering the question, What's this body for? when it had failed, a year before, to have a much longed-for third baby.

At the time I couldn't see this. I believed I was going along to judo because my sons had worn me down with their pestering. For years they had been desperate to take up some vicious killing sport which involved chops to the kidneys and cool Bruce Lee-type headbands. One day after we'd been swimming I consulted the noticeboard at our local leisure centre. 'Look, there's a judo club,' I said. 'Judo's a martial art! Why don't we go along and see what it's like?' I hoped that the thrill of white pyjamas, Japanese terminology and rolling breakfalls would distract them from the fact that they wouldn't be doing any kidney chopping.

The following Saturday afternoon we made

60

our way to the big sports hall where the coach, a man in his late forties, was putting the mats out. I glanced around and saw there was a woman coach too, about ten years younger than me. She seemed busy with some paperwork, so I approached the man. His name was Keith. He looked normal enough, about my height, grey hair buzzed short, no scary ninja tattoos on his face, only one head — yes, I could trust my babies to him. 'Two new ones for you,' I said. He straightened up, looked me in the eye and said, 'Are you coming on the mat, too?' A wholly unexpected YES! surged up inside me. It was his straightforward friendly approach — along with a hint of disrespectful humour — that made me reply, 'OK. If you bring me a suit, I'll join in next week.' It was time to get back in touch with my inner tomboy.

My sons did judo for about a year, then gave it up, the younger one because it was too violent, the older because it was not violent enough. Six years on I'm still doing it. Why? Partly, I'm sure, because I did it as a child. When you get to a certain age, there is no denying that childhood things pack a hefty nostalgic punch. Be that as it may, landing on your back so hard you think your brains are going to shoot out of your ears is a pretty good cure for nostalgia. Dewy-eyed reminiscing can't account for my lasting passion for judo. People often say to me in doubting tones (perhaps eyeing the bruises), 'Well, I suppose it's a good way of keeping fit.' So is Nordic walking. Let's be honest — I'm in it for the fighting. That's the real reason. As a clubmate of mine once remarked, 'I don't feel right in myself if I haven't ripped someone's head off on a Saturday.'

But why fighting? Why do I love it so much? It certainly offers a contrast to the rest of my life. Maybe in recent years I've spent too much time alone with books and ideas, living in my head, not my body, and judo is a way of correcting this imbalance. It wasn't always like that. There's no escaping the physical when you have babies. You are completely mired down in it, all the cuddling and feeding and wiping and rocking and soothing and singing, the whole heroic attempt to wade through daily life with one baby clamped on your bosom, the other round your leg. When my sons were tiny I was desperate for half an hour to myself to read without someone climbing on me. All those years of honing my mind and my biggest intellectual challenge of the day was how to put Action Man's boots on. (The answer is to suck his feet first.) In the midst of all that, I would never have believed that there was such a thing as too much time alone, thinking.

Church is the other significant part of my life, and although it's more sociable than sitting in my study reading and writing, it isn't a whole lot more physical. Apart from the odd barn dance or stampede to the dessert table at a bring-and-share lunch, the most physical contact we get in the C of E is when we are sharing the peace in Holy Communion. This is usually confined to a handshake, or perhaps a peck; but kissing is so easily bungled by socially challenged Anglicans that it's simpler to retreat into your hymn book or start fumbling for your collection money.

So fighting offers a contrast, a spot of yang to go with the yin. It unleashes the killer instincts held in check by the twin domesticating forces of motherhood and the Church of England. Maybe this is why I also find it a great stress-buster. A few years ago as I was driving to judo, I saw a road sign which must originally have read 'DANGER — KEEP OUT'. Half of the letters had fallen off to leave the words, 'ANGER OUT'. Great motto, I thought. Better out than in, where it will gnaw away at your soul. Any vigorous physical exercise can be a way of getting that anger out, whether it be a thrash around on the squash court or knocking up a batch of home-made bread. Wrestling a lump of dough into submission can be extremely satisfying. Imagine, if you will, the pleasure of doing the same to a willing opponent!

It's no good. Even without being able to see your faces, I know that some of you will be wearing expressions of incomprehension tinged with disgust. Each to their own, you are thinking, as if I am describing a mild perversion — nothing illegal, more some kind of mucky fetish.

Maybe it's this simple: either you are a fighter, or you aren't. The midwife who delivered me, seeing me square my shoulders and bawl, apparently said to my mother, 'My word, she's going to be a real fighter!' Was she right? Am I a born fighter? I think I must be, although this puzzles me a bit, considering the lengths I'll go to in my everyday life to avoid confrontation, the amount of pride I am prepared to swallow, the endless mitigating factors and other points of view I will invent in order to excuse my cowardice. I would rather eat bluebottle soup than cause a scene in a restaurant. What I need is a T-shirt which says, 'Oh well, never mind.' Or simply, 'Sorry.' I apologise to people who barge into me. Occasionally, I even apologise to cashpoints and automatic doors.

The problem with being English is that our anger dial isn't very nuanced. It has two settings: on and off. We have nothing between placating and psychotic. After long years as a clergy wife, my rage-ometer gets jammed in the off position. What judo offers, I think, is a safe place to fight. Everyone there knows the score. Aggression can be properly channelled and things won't escalate out of control the way a confrontation in the street might. If someone grabs me by the lapels and roughs me up, I know what it means. It means we're having a *randori*[1] session. It's not personal. It's not an assault. My opponent doesn't hate me, and it won't get out of hand. (Although here's a tip for women players: never approach a male clubmate with the words, 'Come on then, you big wuss.') If it were ever in danger of doing so, I, or the coach watching, could call a halt. '*Matte!*' is one of the first Japanese words you learn. It means 'Stop!'

---

[1] This is free-flowing practice fighting. It is meant to be 'light', as opposed to full-on contest. Normally this means it will be light for approximately three seconds before testosterone kicks in. I'm not being sexist. Women have testosterone, too. How do you think Jolene cream bleach stays in business?

What really frustrates me is my inability to convey to others how much fun judo is. I expect some people are put off by all this fighting talk. On the other hand, most of us have a deep reluctance to believe that any form of physical exercise could be enjoyable. When I lived in Gateshead, ten years ago now, the local leisure centre produced a leaflet called 'Keep Fit the Fun Way'. I doubt if anyone was fooled, any more than they would be by a leaflet at the doctor's called 'Vasectomies the Fun Way'. This was the first time in my life when keeping fit (for which read: *Losing Weight*) had become an issue. I'd just had my second baby, and was feeling extremely put out that the weight wasn't dropping off while I breastfed, the way people promised it would. Breastfeeding — Nature's liposuction. If only. Eventually I admitted I was going to have to do something about shifting the weight, or embrace blimphood forever. To be honest, I look back on this as my fat-bloke era, when trackie bottoms teamed with oversized rugby shirts and DM's seemed like a funky fashion statement.

Let's be brutal. When it comes to weight loss, there are only two options:[1] Eat Less, or

---

[1] With the obvious exception of amoebic dysentery.

Do More. Temperamentally, I've always found the latter slightly more appealing. Embracing something is better than renunciation, I always think. Especially if it means renouncing cake. This was why I used to drag myself along to a step aerobics class. I can report that the leaflet was lying: it was *never* fun. I never enjoyed it. Many people did, but on the whole they tended to be the ones perving from the gallery that ran the full length of the sports hall. My husband played squash at the same leisure centre and on one occasion he came out of the changing room and was swept along in a stampede of blokes. 'Is there a match on or something?' he asked, rushing to keep up. 'No — ladies' keep-fit class!'

'Steps' for me involved galumphing about at the back of the class trying to copy the women in front. It was a horrible flashback to the ballet classes I took as a nine-year-old. We were led by an enthusiastic young *Oberstleutnant* called Steph, who shouted instructions into one of those pop-singer microphones attached to her head. The only real improvement was that she wasn't shouting in French. Having said that, my grasp of Geordie was a bit rudimentary, too. Sometimes I couldn't even understand my own children, like the time when my younger son

67

asked me to draw him a wheel. 'Sure, what kind? A car wheel? A tractor wheel?' 'Noo-ah! A *killer* wheel!' Even when I did understand the instructions I was always turning an ankle on the step or going hop-step instead of step-hop, and sneakily attempting to do star jumps with my knees clamped together.[1] The only bit I almost liked was the stomach exercises. They provided a welcome opportunity to lie on the floor.

Exercise for most women is a grim and solitary business — the running treadmill, the slow lane at the swimming pool (with your head out of the water because of your mascara), the exercise bike. Classes are solitary, too. Even if you go with friends, you will still each be locked in your own private misery. Men are much more likely to do some kind of competitive sport, like squash, or a team game. And they are much more likely to come back from their bout of exercise having had a good laugh, having *enjoyed* themselves.

On the whole, women don't expect to encounter the words 'exercise' and 'enjoy' in the same sentence. Exercise is our penance for all those Danish pastries and glasses of wine. It is our own fault we are fat, therefore it is only proper that we suffer. Diet and

---

[1] Ask any woman who has given birth.

exercise are suitable punishments. Or rather, they *will* be — starting from next week. I mean it. From next week, off to the gym and no more booze or empty carbs.

Judo breaks out of this nightmare cycle of guilt and self-indulgence. Sometimes I practically sob with relief when I remember that I will never, ever have to go to an aerobics class again. It's as good as waking up from those exam dreams where you have forgotten to revise. I will never again have to feel like a dyspraxic tractor, never need leggings, or a thong leotard, or anything made of pink towelling. Give judo a go! Remember the baggy white pyjamas, so kind to the fuller figure in a world of unforgiving Lycra sports gear! Listen, judo is not like swimming. You won't have to put off starting until you've lost a bit of weight. Beef is good. As the Bible says, 'Let your soul delight itself in fatness' (Isaiah, 55:2b) — a scripture verse and a hymn for every occasion, that is my promise to you.

And remember, too, that if anyone does happen to perv at you, you will know how to break his arm.

★　★　★

After we moved from Gateshead to Walsall I gave up on aerobics. For a while I did no exercise at all, but guilt and weight anxiety finally prompted me to have another go at running. It is a different game when you are twenty years older and three stone heavier. Ten miles? How had I ever run that far? Had I really enjoyed it? It seemed inconceivable. I made a couple of attempts, trudging round the streets near where we lived, but I gave up after I was yodelled at by a group of gonad-driven oiks in Walsall's arboretum. Running is humiliating enough for a big woman without a spotty teenager snickering, 'Look at them tits wobbling up and down!' '*Those* tits, you illiterate moron!' I yelled back. No I didn't. I'm too polite, and anyway, I didn't have enough breath. I also didn't stick up two fingers at them. This is surely one of the worst things about being married to a vicar, never being able to give people the V-sign, in case they show up in church one day.

Things changed when I encountered the Atkins diet and lost enough weight to feel happier in my running kit. (And in my body, if I'm honest.) Still, I am never going to be much of a runner. I don't have the right physique. I neither have the powerful frame of a sprinter, nor the whippet-like leanness of a distance runner; I'm just woman-shaped. Despite this, running somehow became a habit. If I think of running the straight race now, I see it as something dutiful. It's about carrying on, nothing flashy, nothing brilliant. I'm no longer expecting to come first. It's a matter of plodding on. If I don't stop, eventually I'll reach the winning post. It's even possible to admire the view along the way.

Apart from judo, running is the only form of exercise I do these days. I don't count walking. Walking, for me, is simply a way of getting out of driving. I drive like a complete girl, hunched praying over the wheel, forgetting to breathe when I am overtaking on motorways and colliding with stationary objects at speeds of under 5mph. In fact, I backed into a bollard outside church only last year. Hearing the crump, several members of the congregation sprang forward at once to guide me into the parking space, helpfully pointing out the bollard. *Yes, yes, I know it's there* now, *don't I?* I thought, smiling in that clenched way they teach clergy spouses at theological college. (ANGER IN!)[1]

---

[1] Funnily enough, the curate's husband hit the very same bollard several weeks later. He too was assisted by members of the congregation who appeared just as he was pounding the steering wheel. 'I couldn't even swear!' he lamented. Welcome to the Clergy Spouses Club, brother.

When I run, I try to switch off my inner narrator, the one who notes what the birds and the weather are doing, and comes up with moving similes for tree bark. Instead, I try to listen to my body. Sports people are supposed to do this. Paula Radcliffe tells us in her autobiography that for once she didn't listen to her body during the Athens Olympics, and look what happened. Unfortunately, when I listen to my body it says things like 'Oh, please don't make me!' and 'Can I have a doughnut?'

There are ways of tackling this very natural reluctance. For a start, I never run very far. These days it's usually three miles. A few years back it was between a mile and a half and two miles, taking a meandering route back from dropping my younger son off at school. There was a tiny plus first thing in the morning: I could fling on some running gear and not bother with a shower and hair wash. This small piece of laziness was enough to overcome the much larger laziness of not wanting to run at all. Go *with* your grain, not against it, I say. By the time I reached the school gates, self-esteem did not permit me to wimp out. Everyone had seen me arrive in running kit and been impressed. I could not therefore walk home. You see how I cleverly harnessed the two mortal sins of sloth and pride and made them work for me?

There are many rewards for running, and that's what keeps me doing it. Firstly, it builds up stamina, always important for judo, especially if you are a veteran like me and come up against youngsters with boundless energy. Boundless energy and spots. Hah! Spots and exams *and* student loans. Gosh, I'm glad I'm old.

Secondly, there is the chemical reward of the endorphin rush, your body's own morphine. Basically, I run because I can't afford heroin. I'm aware of the dangers of getting hooked, of course. When I catch myself flogging the kids' computer games to finance my trainer-buying habit, I promise I will seek help.

Thirdly, you will eventually get more muscular, and a muscular physique burns off more calories than a fat one, so you can get away with the odd biscuit-fest. I have no idea why women are so terrified of becoming muscly. What are they imagining? Two reckless sessions at the gym and WHOOMPH! — biceps exploding out of your arms like airbags? Relax. Big muscles require testosterone in quantities most of us girls simply don't have. If you are struggling to grow a decent moustache, rest assured that you can pump iron with impunity. You will not end up like an Eastern bloc shotputter before random drugs testing was imposed. You will end up looking fab.

As a short cut to a muscular physique, there is always the gym. I did some strength training a while back because I was the only woman in our club at that stage, and I got fed up with being tossed about like a rag doll. Giving way was all very well. If I was ever going to fight back effectively, I needed to be stronger. Up till that point, I had never been inside a gym, I'd only sneered from the outside. Knowing myself well, I admitted that there was no point in taking out expensive gym membership and only going twice. Who wants to bankroll those mad-eyed gym bunnies? What I needed was a pay-as-you-go system.

Our local municipal leisure centre came up trumps. I went along to 'Mint Condition' at Walsall's Gala Baths for an induction session, after which I was deemed competent to use the various pieces of gym equipment. That was the theory. However, the person demonstrating was an Olympic speed mumbler, and I didn't like to ask him to repeat himself. There were two blokes being inducted at the same time, and they kept nodding and saying, 'OK, right, got that,' so I'd have felt foolish asking for clarification.

As I should have foreseen, I ended up

feeling far more foolish later on. I turned up for my first session, stared at the machines and didn't have a clue what to do. I never did get up the nerve to try running on the treadmill, in case it fired me straight through the plate-glass window on to the street below. Weights, I decided with a haughty sniff. That's what I'm here for. I get my aerobic exercise elsewhere. Gradually, by a combination of covertly watching other gym users and reading the notices on the walls out of the corner of my eye, I got the hang of it. Or at least, I thought I did. One morning I found an older gentleman standing alarmingly close to me and breathing hard through his nose, watching as I did my biceps curls.

'Yow'm cheating, yow am,' he informed me after a while. 'Yow'm bending yer legs. When I was in the army they taught us — '

Well, we're not *in* the army now, *are* we? I thought. So piss off and leave me alone. It was my nutter magnet at work again, that sign on my forehead which reads, 'Come and patronise and bore me! I'm too polite to escape!' Anyone slightly bonkers within a fifty-mile radius is drawn to it. Trains and buses are the worst. It is frequently coupled with the conviction that my new friend 'knows me from somewhere'. 'I've seen you somewhere before, haven't I?' they say.

But to return to the gym.

Actually, I can't. It burnt down, and the council hasn't seen fit to rebuild it. I expect their reasoning is that the local population gets all the physical exercise they need while vomit-skating in the town centre after the bars close. I've taken to pinching my older son's weights instead, and doing my arm exercises at my bedroom window when I get back from my run.

The other thing I use is my trusty ab-roller. You may remember seeing these advertised in all the weekend colour supplements with a picture of a suntanned bloke carrying a woman in a yellow bikini. (The woman being the one in the bikini.) 'I went down two dress sizes in fifteen minutes!' she simpered. 'Target your lower abdomen! five minutes a day! It really works!' Cobblers! we all scoffed, before sending off for one. They retailed at around £39.99 back then, but I discovered you could get them from Steve's in Walsall, next to the bus station, for £4.95. Regardless of how much you pay for them, they last about four months before the main spring goes with an almighty twang, sending a handy jolt of adrenalin through your entire system first thing in the morning. Four months probably doesn't strike you as a very long lifespan for a piece of exercise equipment. I'm reliably informed they last for years if they are stored on top of a wardrobe. The manufacturers have shrewdly gambled on the fact that their merchandise only needs to be robust enough to outlast the average New Year's resolution.

We are often told that keeping fit is a question of building exercise into your daily routine. This is why I swear by my ab-roller. A few rolls on the kitchen floor first thing while your coffee brews. As the actress said to the bishop.[1] Once you get into the habit, it's no bother. The roller does half the work for you. It's not like sit-ups, which I loathe almost as much as press-ups. I don't *do* press-ups, I used to say in my princess voice. Keith always reassured me that half press-ups were just as good, but Neil at the club used to jeer, 'You've got your knees on the mat!' I simply ignored him. These days I can just manage fifteen full press-ups before my eyeballs burst from their sockets and drop on the floor.

So here's my advice: if you find going to

_____

[1] I know a bishop who went into an off-licence once, and spotted a jeroboam of champagne. 'My! That's a big one!' he heard himself remark. 'As the actress said to . . . the . . . ' began the assistant cheerily, before noting the purple shirt and tailing off.

the gym simply isn't possible, either physically or emotionally, don't despair. Work out at home. I've found it's cheaper, more convenient and, unless we have house guests, no nutters approach me. I can watch the birds in the back garden while I exercise — chaffinches, blue tits, the occasional goldcrest and heron. Once there was a wood pigeon sitting on her nest in the big Douglas fir, at about eye level. She stared at me. I got the feeling she knew me from somewhere.

Some Useful Tips for Useless Runners

- if you have a big chest, wear *two* sports bras (an ordinary one with a tight cropped top bra over the top), especially if you are a woman
- spit either to the left or right, otherwise you will run into your own flob
- run with your mouth open, it dries your saliva, so you won't need to spit
- close your mouth when approaching a cloud of insects
- respect large dogs
- kick small dogs from your path
- a double espresso enables you to train 30 per cent harder and kicks the body straight into fat-burning mode. (If you have a weak

bladder it also helps you sprint the last 100 metres home)

- remember: *running is always worth it*

Yes, running is worth it, but it's no longer my dominant life metaphor. These days it's all about fighting.

Getting Your Yellow Belt

When I was a youngster, yellow belt was as far as I got. It felt pretty impressive at the time, but to tell the truth, getting your yellow belt as a senior isn't that difficult, really. Assuming you've survived your first session and are undeterred by the thought of landing on your back underneath a fat sweaty bloke who proceeds to break your arm and throttle you, you will soon be ready to take your first grade. You can do this in your own club with your coach examining you on your techniques. These fall basically into two categories: standing work (i.e. throwing) and groundwork (grappling, pin-downs, armlocks and strangles).

The yellow-belt throw is *o-goshi*, which we encountered in the previous chapter. The first time you experience *o-goshi*, you may well shriek. You will find yourself being picked up and rolled over someone's hip head first (or so it feels) onto the floor. If the person throwing you is over six foot, it's a long way to fall. Newcomers to judo are often scared of being thrown by a black belt. It isn't long before you realise how very much worse it is to be thrown by a novice, particularly one attempting their first *o-goshi*. Whereas a black belt will control your landing (unless you have annoyed them), a beginner will dump you like a sack of spuds. Well, we all have to start somewhere, so if you are a higher grade paired with a novice in a training session, you just have to be a good sport and let them do it, and say, 'Good throw!' (Or give them a thumbs up if you are too winded to speak.)

For your groundwork you will need to know one pin-down technique and one armlock, but there is little point in describing them here. It would be like giving origami instruction over the phone. After successfully demonstrating *kuzure-kesa-gatame* and *ude-garame* (don't worry, the terms soon become second nature) you will be asked to translate four simple refereeing terms from Japanese into English. This is where swots have an advantage. The skills you learned cramming for exams never really leave you, and you'll be able to rattle off the list ('begin', 'stop', 'a hold is on', 'hold broken') without difficulty.

And that's it: you are a 9th kyu. Easy-peasy lemon squeezy. Your coach will sign up your licence and you can go to the sports shop and buy yourself a yellow belt.

After this, there are two aspects to progress in judo: theory and contest. Your coach will continue to test you on your theory and sign your licence, but after yellow you will need to win your belt by defeating an opponent at a grading. Buoyed up by your success in moving up from white to yellow, you may well want to get on with the theory ready for your first proper contest. 'How far have you got your theory signed up?' we ask one another. If the answer is 'Up to 1st kyu', you know that you are dealing with someone fairly advanced or utterly deluded, since 1st kyu is the one below black belt.

While you are still a yellow belt, then, you will do your theory in preparation for orange belt. For this you need to demonstrate two new throws. The first, called 'tsuri-komi-goshi', ('lift-pull hip throw'), is one you will probably never use again, outside of formal demonstration, as it's difficult and it kills your arm. Everyone grumbles about this technique and we never tire of being amazed that it should be included at this relatively early stage in the syllabus. The second, o-uchi-gari, is a nifty little throw where you 'reap' your opponent's leg out from beneath him or her. '*Gari*' throws are contrasted with '*gake*' throws, the latter involving a hooking action, rather than sweeping, or 'reaping' the leg away. We once had a black belt from the Kodokan in Tokyo training at our club and he carefully explained *gake* to me: 'Cath — fook leg, not leap. Fooking, OK?' And you know what? Ever since then 'fooking judo' is something I have often thought. In case you are tut-tutting at this non-PC sniggering at Japanese English, let me point out that Daisuki sniggered at our Japanese. He was particularly amused by *mune-gatami*, which we translate as 'chest hold'. Apparently 'tit hold' is nearer the mark.

The groundwork technique for orange is 'Escape from between an opponent's legs'.[1] You will have to show knowledge of refereeing calls and contest rules. Finally, you will be asked to name three 'prohibited acts'. These are listed in the back of the BJA syllabus booklet, under 'Article 28 of the BJA Contest Rules' and 'Appendix Article 28 — Prohibited Acts'.

---

[1] When I told my husband I had been learning this, he asked, 'Why would you *want* to?' This line of speculation is very unhelpful in a mixed club, see below.

As you would anticipate, prohibited acts incur penalties. These range from 'slight infringement' (the ref will point at the offending player and call 'Shido!') through 'serious infringement' ('Chui!') to 'grave infringement' and, finally, 'very grave infringement', which will result in instant disqualification: 'Hansoku make!' This would be incurred if you employed some highly dangerous technique such as diving head first onto the mat, or wearing a 'hard or metallic object (covered or not)'. In theory, metal bra hooks can get you disqualified. I confess that I take a walk on the wild side on this one, and from what I have seen in the changing rooms, I am not alone. So far there have been no spot checks. Crop-top metal-free sports bras are useless to those of us needing a bit of support. Obviously, I wouldn't wear an underwired bra. You could take someone's eye out if one of those babies blew under pressure. I expect that is what the BJA is hoping to guard against. In this litigious age they don't want to be bankrupted by a rash of lingerie-related compensation claims.

There is also the whole issue of the 'Spirit of Judo' to bear in mind. Proper formal etiquette is hugely important. You may be penalised for any act deemed to be 'Against the Spirit of Judo'. So no gobbing or swearing. This is no problem for me, as I am not terribly good at either, despite decades of secret practice, but for others it can be a real hardship. At a recent competition a bloke was being taunted by spectators. He lost it, stormed off the mat, went and headbutted a heckler, then came back on to resume his contest. '*Hansoku make!*' Disqualified. Apparently, he should have bowed before leaving the mat.

How to Fall Properly

I feel bad about this as I should have mentioned it earlier. Still, so long as you haven't been trying out throws on anyone, it won't matter. One of the very first things you are taught in judo is how to fall in such a way as to minimise injury. 'Breakfalls', we call them. It's important to practise them every training session, even if you really, *really* don't feel like it, for age- or alcohol-related reasons. There are different types: backwards, side, front and those diving kamikaze forward rolls that people associate with martial arts. The Japanese word for it is *ukemi*.

Kano summarises *ukemi* for us like this: 'The main points to bear in mind when falling are to strike the mat hard with one or both arms, to curve the back, and to tuck in the chin so that your head does not hit the mat.' If you practise breakfalls for long enough, they make their way into your muscle memory. This is a good thing, because to start with it's all a bit counter-intuitive. Your instinct, when falling, is to stick out a hand. This is a good way of breaking a wrist, as many players know to their cost. Strike the mat hard with one or both arms, like the man says. I expect this is something to do with Newton and every action having an equal and opposite reaction, but it's a long time since my physics O level, so I honestly wouldn't know. What I do know is that it works. It will sting, but better to have smarting hands than land splat on your back and not be able to breathe for five minutes.

People sometimes ask me if I have ever needed to use my judo in real life. I tell them, 'Yes.' They are disappointed to learn that I am talking about break-falls, rather than the number of cudgel-wielding hoodlums I have dispatched. (I remain confident that judo would be useful under such circumstances, though. Uyenishi, one of the first Japanese experts to arrive in England at the turn of the last century, promoted judo partly because he felt it would help to 'secure young English ladies against any danger resulting from ruffianly attack'.) One day when I was about twelve I thought it would be fun to play circus clowns, so I got my younger sister Ruth to feed my stilts up my trouser legs. All was going well until I paused to consider my dismount and fell in a slow scything motion onto the pavement. Remembering my judo, I turned my head to one side and took the fall on both forearms rather than my face. Muscle memory, you see. If I had stuck out my hands, I might well have broken my wrists falling from that height. I learned from this. I have never stuck stilts up my trouser legs since.

Much more recently, I tripped coming out of our front door and found myself hurtling across the drive getting closer to the ground with every pace. I had time to remember to tuck and roll. Anyone walking past would have seen me explode out of my house, execute a swift martial arts roll, before leaping up, dusting off my hands and getting into the car. Hah! In the vicarage, we go shopping this-a-way!

The only time when you might override your newly acquired breakfalling skills is during a contest. Sometimes the sound of a mighty smacking of the mat triggers a Pavlovian reaction in the ref, who will shoot up a hand and cry '*Ippon!*', even if your opponent's technique wasn't a winning throw at all. Some coaches advise their players not to breakfall for this reason. It's a question of weighing up pain against the need to win, really. Work out what is right for you. I'd go with the breakfall every time, personally.

At your first judo session you watch the others somersaulting across the mat. You see them take walloping landings and leap straight back up. I'll never be able to do that, you think. Nevertheless, you try your first tentative head-over-heels. 'Well done!' says your coach. 'Now try and roll over your shoulder, not your head.' You have another go and smack the mat gingerly with your hand, feeling like a right twit. But practice makes perfect. Or adequate, at any rate. You see the point of all this rolling and smacking when eventually — unbelievably! — you reach the stage when you are no longer afraid of being thrown. You may not like it, but it won't actually terrify you. This was quite liberating for me as an adult, as I'd been getting increasingly sissy with each passing year. One of the unmistakable signs of middle age is thinking 'Oh no!' rather than 'Hooray!' when you see it's been snowing. As in, 'Oh no, I bet it's really slippery underfoot.' As a child I was keen on rough and tumble — head-over-heels races down steep hills, clumsy cartwheels across the playground. Tripping over was a nuisance in games of tag or netball, but you got up and carried on running. It's just not like that as an adult. I read somewhere that an adult twice the height of a child falls not with twice but with *eight times* the impact. Newton again, probably. Something to do with mass? No wonder it hurts.

I was explaining this to my older son one icy morning on the way to school. 'What — like that, you mean?' he asked, interested, as my feet shot out from underneath me and I fell flat on my back. (It was his gruff way of saying, 'Goodness! Are you all right, Mum?') This time I was saved from serious injury not by judo, but by my younger son's school backpack which I was carrying, and my embarrassing furry hat. *Damn! Forgot to breakfall. Forgot to tuck my chin in.* I'm still cross with myself about that. I got whiplash and couldn't train for a fortnight.

When I took up judo again after my (almost) thirty-year lay-off, I could vividly remember how fearless I was as a child on the mat, how I used to run and dive headlong into my rolling breakfalls. Was I ever going to do that again? Unlikely. I was reaching the age where I thought twice about even sitting on the floor, let alone hurling myself onto it. My joints were too stiff, I didn't bounce or roll the way I used to. I'd even noticed myself going 'Oof!' when I lowered myself onto a sofa, and grunting as I levered myself back up. It looked an awfully long way down onto that mat.

But I started gently, rolling from my knees and gradually working up to a crouching start. The key is being able to relax into it. If you relax, it hurts less. I guess my breakfalls are as clumsy as my cartwheels always used to be, but they are good enough. I can do backward ones, too, but only in batches of three. I believe Newton stated that an adult twice the height of a child will be sick eight times faster if they get dizzy.

★　★　★

I promised in the last chapter that we would be discussing underwear. You have been very patient. I realise now that there are other clothing issues we need to address, so here is the judo equivalent of *What Not to Wear*.

Obviously, you will need to wear your judo suit. Those of you who have watched judo on the TV will have spotted that suits actually come in two different colours — the traditional white, and a bright royal blue. This makes it easier for the referees to work out which player is doing what. Even then it isn't always straightforward. Currently at British Judo Association gradings you have to wear a white suit. Players are differentiated by belt colour. One will wear white, the other red. Contests are announced something like this: 'Vast Bloke-Woman in white, Catherine Fox in red.' Sometimes it's blue instead of red. I've given up trying to understand this. I just do as I'm told.

There are white suits and white suits, mind you. Most people start off with a cheap basic suit, probably imported from Japan. Mine is a *Ki-ai* suit, according to the label; '*ki*' being the Japanese version of '*chi*' (the Chinese word for energy). *Ki-ai* is the martial arts shout you make while executing a technique, or slipping a disc. It's worth practising your *kiai*, if only to train yourself out of the habit of giggling (or muttering that useful Japanese word *Fook!*).

I have a second white suit which I bought in New Zealand. This one is tighter. Tighter is better. It gives my opponent less to grab hold of. It is also more flattering, though this is relative. There is a gap in the market for judo jackets with princess seams. It is possible to spend a huge amount of money on a judo kit. Many players wear Adidas suits, which have lapels of steel that make strangles with the collar nigh on impossible. There is talk of banning this kind of thing. You can always spot a stiff jacket. It will have bloodstains where people have lost the skin off their knuckles trying to get purchase on it.[1] My third suit is a nice blue one which my husband kindly bought me as a Christmas present. Bloodstains don't show up so much on blue suits. Brown really doesn't work with royal blue, though, so all the more reason to keep going for my black belt.

Women players are supposed to wear a plain white T-shirt under their jacket. This is strictly enforced at gradings. You may be the best fighter on the mat, but if you have a Betty Boop T-shirt on, you will be disqualified. Keith once told us that women judo players in Malta go commando. There then followed a period of dreamy speculative silence as the men in the club imagined they were Maltese. (Actually, Keith mentions this fact quite regularly, but my clubmates always seem happy enough to hear it.) Men sometimes wear hoodies or long-sleeved shirts under their jackets during training, which I suppose is to work up a sweat, or some other piece of arcane macho nonsense.

---

[1] Hint: even cheap suits can be made stiff by drying them on a radiator and not using fabric softener.

As far as I can see they never seem to have much trouble sweating without the extra layer. Naturally, this is because they work twenty times harder than us mere females, rather than because they have twenty times more sweat glands per inch of skin. Just roll your eyes and agree. You don't want bloke sweat flicked in your face for answering back.

Now then: underwear. Bras we have already discussed, so on to knickers. The rule is this: white suit, white drawers. Black ones show through. (I once saw a woman getting changed ready for a grading. 'I'm wearing my lucky pants,' she announced to her friend. These appeared to be nylon leopard-print with black lace edging. Perhaps she was hoping for some kind of luck transfer from another area of her life.) I also recommend 100 per cent cotton. Nylon will result in what I am reliably informed is called 'jock rash'. What would the female equivalent be? Thong rash? Ah, yes — word of warning: the judo mat is no place for thongs. Trousers will occasionally come untied, or even get ripped, in the heat of contest. The sensible player lays aside the Agent Provocateurs — and if you are a man, this is even more sensible — and dons white M&S pants.

What not to wear. Glasses. Take them off and get contact lenses. Technically, you don't need to be able to see to do judo, but the world is a bewildering place if you are as short-sighted as I am. I used to hate swimming for this reason. I had an awful fear of wandering into the blokes' changing rooms by accident. Not that I'd have been able to see anything interesting when I got there. Soft contact lenses are better than hard or gas permeable, as they hardly ever get dislodged. It has only happened to me once in four years of fighting. I contemplated laser surgery at one stage, but then I read somewhere that the flap of cornea can come unstuck again if you get a blow to the head, so it seemed to me that this wasn't the best option for the judo player.

Also to be avoided are false nails and make-up of any kind, apart from waterproof mascara (Maybelline's 'Sky High Curves' goes into total meltdown, I happen to know). I once fought a woman at a grading who was wearing foundation. After the bout, one of my clubmates told me I looked as if I'd been attacked by the Rimmel counter at Boots.

Personally I think long hair is folly, too. Remember, 'no metal objects (covered or not)'. Although nobody checks bra hooks, they scrupulously check hairbands and make you remove any that contain even the tiniest scrap of metal, so you will be forced to use a scrunchy or nylon band that slips out the whole time. I keep my hair short. 'As short as you think I can go,' I tell my stylist, Andy, from Francesco's Walsall, 'without it looking scary.' 'Without making you look like a big butch bull dyke,' he clarifies helpfully. Off the mat I do aim to retain a certain feisty femininity. Lara Croft is a useful role model here. She teaches us that it is OK to be posh, have a PhD *and* curves. And if anyone quibbles, just blow them up with a bazooka.

Diary

2 April 2005

The night before the grading and I feel sick. We spent the last week near Eastbourne staying in a cottage near my parents-in-law. *Welcome to the Sunshine Coast!* said the signs. The first day was sunny, then we had rain and fog until the morning we set off, when the sun reappeared. *The Sunshine Coast Gives You Two Fingers!*

I couldn't shake off the inner gloom, either. I've been desperately weepy and anxious, despite the St John's wort tablets. Wait — think how bad it would have been *without* the St John's wort! Can't help remembering this time last year, and how different 2005 was looking then. I burst into tears as I led the intercessions in church on Easter Day. Pete says this is OK, and not too much for the congregation, so long as I don't mind the spread betting on how long I'm going to last without crying whenever I lead the prayers. I always do it. I thought I was going to be safe on Easter of all days, but no. You just can't unpick the joy from the pain and keep them separate.

Things aren't much better now we're back, although the gloom is lifting a bit to make way for abject terror. I'm sitting up here in my study with a cup of peppermint tea to settle my stomach. Pete and the boys have been trying to cheer me up. They are going to come along and support me tomorrow, which I've now decided will help me, but not if they come and talk to me. I may go and talk to them, but it is to be at my initiative. We had a group hug, the kind we usually have when Pete and I are trying to have a couple hug, and get gatecrashed.

The kit is washed and ironed. The lucky New Zealand T-shirt is getting a bit bobbly and worn, and the lucky trousers are wearing thin. I've been feeling the same sick nerves I felt before my last night at the Wellington dojo, when I knew Kevin would give me a line-up. Then he got stranded in Auckland by bad weather, so it wasn't as bad as I'd feared. I didn't fight the whole club, just the higher grades, and they let me do groundwork. So don't worry! It'll be fine!

I've let it become too important in my mind. It's because it's my first DAN GRADING. Whereas, in fact, it doesn't really matter. The last grading had more riding on it, as I needed two outright wins to grade up. This time it's a question of just having a go and seeing if I manage to get any points towards my black belt. Barring injury, the worst that will happen is not winning any bouts. Which is OK. Surely I can be OK with this? I'm letting myself be haunted by the scary psycho teenagers, who may well not be there, let's face it (setting aside the attractive thought that, for all I know, I may feature as the big scary old psycho GI Jane in their imaginations). As Pete helpfully pointed out, there may well be seven rubbish brown belts out there. There will certainly be several anxious women somewhere in the region tonight, wishing like me it could all be over, that they didn't have to go through with it.

And of course, I don't. I'm the only one making me do this. It's like finals, only voluntary. I've been going through all those 'If I broke my arm now/the Second Coming happened, I wouldn't have to do it' thoughts. Followed by the mature reflection that I'd only have to do it later. Which would mean I'd wasted a perfectly good week of misery all for no reason.

There are parallels with my doctorate, too. Looking back, it was misery. I remember the awful night when I thought I'd missed my submission date. My teeth were chattering with dread. It was a long hard grind, but like the Good Book almost says, all that was forgotten in the joy that a PhD has been awarded. I know I shall feel the same when I get my black belt. I will reread this and laugh (kindly, gently, of course) at my silly fears, and how I couldn't shrug them off. This time tomorrow it will be over. Then I will only have to go to another four or five, and it will be *really* over.

Pete tells me I don't have to be strong for his sake. He says this because I told him that my inner voices suddenly asked me in a tender but slightly exasperated way, *Whatever made you think you had to be strong?* To atone for all the times when I know I'm weak, when I am powerless to prevent the worst happening. I know in my head that there was nothing at all I could do to hang on to that baby last year. Not my fault. Just one of those things. But oh. This is the time of anniversary, a year on from the pregnancy, and the panicked anxiety I felt all through last summer after the miscarriage has reared up again. And none of this can be readily untangled from the judo. *Here's something my body can do.* This will be true tomorrow. Yes, I can go out there and fight, and maybe win. My body can do this. It just wasn't supposed to be this way.

3 April 2005
Done, thank God. Here's something I've learned in this life: everything passes. It passes,

then it fades. Arrived at about 8.45 at the new judo centre. Not many there. My licence was first in the 'ladies' 1st kyu pile, and it remained the only one there till gone 9.45, by which time I was trembling with relief that I'd be able to withdraw honourably. Heather and Jo were there, though Debbie was ill. Found Keith, who was keeping me distracted with funny stories, until he noticed I was away, glazed-eyed, on Planet Dread, and aborted his anecdote till another time. I apologised.

Every so often I went back to the check-in desk to see if there were any more licences, and saw a bloke adding his to the 1st kyu pile. Then a moment of pure horror — not a bloke, but a big scary woman, considerably taller and brawnier than me. If it's just the two of us, I'm definitely withdrawing, I thought. Keith went to recce, and came back with the news that she was going for her 2nd dan. Nearly wept with relief. He'd checked her weight and it was nearly 90kg. I was a mere 69kg this time.

Just as I was about to give up and go and get my fee refunded, an examiner called my name. Two more had signed in, so we were on. We bowed on to the far mat with the men's 3rd dan fighters. The other two women both seemed very nice, and I can't tell you how much difference that makes. We'd deliberated for several minutes about withdrawing, as one of the others was an undergraduate and felt £7.50 per fight was a bit steep. We were all waiting for someone else to decide, and in the end one of them said, 'Sod it, we're here now. We may as well fight.'

OK. Two fights, then. The others were called up first. The undergraduate won with a pin-down at the end of a very long bout. However, she injured her finger in the process, which meant that when I put on a good strangle on her, she couldn't pull me off, so I won nice and quickly. Pete and the boys were in the gallery looking down, but silent, as they didn't know what to shout. I could hear the twins and Keith from the far corner yelling, 'Come on, Cath!'

My second opponent was a student teacher, and we eventually drew, though not before she'd been awarded a *waza-ari*, only to have it immediately overturned. Then a fourth contestant turned up, having mistakenly gone to the Samurai Club in Kidderminster. She and the teacher fought. The teacher pinned her down and won. Then I fought the new girl, feeling I had a chance, but she armlocked me as I tried to escape from a pin-down. Hah. A move I've often used myself. My elbow is quite sore now, as is my neck, but here I am. It's done. It passed. It will fade. I hope that with this grading out of the way, it will simply be a slog, not a hideous ordeal. So it was 10 points apiece on the 'ladies' 1st kyu mat. Only 60 more points to go. I will train like mad. I will get there in the end. Be thou strong and very courageous, as the Good Book says.

3

Orange Belt

Jesus wants me for a sunbeam,
To shine for Him each day;
In every way try to please Him
At home, at school, at play.
A sunbeam, a sunbeam,
Jesus wants me for a sunbeam;
A sunbeam, a sunbeam
I'll be a sunbeam for Him.

Hymn 1129, 'I'll be a Sunbeam'
in *Sacred Songs and Solos*

Judo and the Traditional Vicar's Wife

A few years back I wrote three novels. Whenever I was interviewed about them, a couple of questions always came up. One was 'What does you husband think of your books?' If I'd been a bit more clued up about publicity I might have known to say, 'Don't ask! He thinks they are immoral and

102

shocking. Goodness *knows* what will happen if the bishop finds out!' Instead, I mouthed something bland and un-newsworthy about how supportive he was. This was faithfully reported under the headline 'PEW! WHAT A SCORCHER!'

The second question was 'Are you a traditional vicar's wife?' I took this to mean 'Do you wear twinsets and sensible shoes and rule the flower rota with a rod of iron?' and of course, the answer is 'No'. I don't do any of those things. Nor do I teach in the Sunday school, go door-to-door collecting, or organise jumble sales. I don't launder the altar linen, crochet gonks, or call upon ailing parishioners with jars of my nourishing calf's-foot jelly. I do bake cakes, but only in an ironic postmodern way. I have been known to make sandwiches for people who call at the vicarage hoping for the train fare to Glasgow, but occasionally I refuse. 'Are you telling me to piss off?' demanded one disgruntled caller. 'Well, yes, actually, I am,' I replied. 'You're not as nice as the last people who lived here!' he shouted. 'I only came because you've got a cross in the window.' I'll soon get rid of *that*, I thought, shutting the door.

In case you are wondering what happened to the parable of the Good Samaritan here, this particular man was about six foot three, drunk, with a history of violence, just out of prison and I was in the house alone with two small children. I still felt bad about it afterwards, though. In this respect, at least, I am a traditional vicar's wife. We are extremely talented at feeling bad about things. Guilt is our default mode, our mental screensaver.

So what is it like being a vicar's wife? I find this a bit tricky to answer. I have nothing to compare it with, as I've never been a wife of anything else. (Or I hadn't, until Pete became canon chancellor at Lichfield Cathedral last year. Still, it's the same thing, with bells on.) We got married after graduating, then moved to Cambridge, where he began his training for the ministry. I can't even give a proper answer to the question, 'What did you think when you found out he was going to be a vicar?' since the first words I ever heard him utter were, 'I'm going to be a vicar.' I believe this was a chat-up line. God moves in mysterious ways.

Theological college turned out to be an excellent preparation for vicarage life. In our first week at Ridley Hall, one of my husband's fellow ordinands approached me and said, 'You're someone's wife, aren't you?' Since that day, this has been my public role — to be Someone's Wife, not a person in my own right. Only the other week as I crossed the

Cathedral Close someone called out, 'Morning, Mrs Chancellor!' It would be a strange woman who did not rebel from time to time. I'm sure it's this that prompts me to write 'ARSE' with other people's alphabet fridge magnets, then blame it on my sons. At one stage I used to wear Doc Martens, but they gradually became de rigueur for feisty young clergy wives of a certain stamp, so I stopped. Nowadays I wear four-inch stiletto-heeled thigh boots. I just wanted to tell you that, not because I really do, but because it sounds so much more exotic than the truth, which is that I have to wear sensible footwear because of my poorly toe.[1] If there is such a thing as a stereotypical vicar's wife you need to look beyond the clothes (not twinsets, by the way, so much as eighties Laura Ashley worn with navy tights and court shoes) into the heart and mind. At the extreme end of the spectrum you will find a *very* angry woman. She will probably be depressed, because she can find no acceptable outlet for her anger. She can't be angry when her husband is out every night and never takes time off, because he is doing God's work. She can't shout,

---

[1] Hereinafter and for evermore to be referred to as my 'Foot Injury', in keeping with what I observe to be good martial arts practice.

'What about ME?!' because everything he does is so *worthy*. If she was brought up as an evangelical (the correct term for the happy-clappy trendy vicar wing of the church) her problems will be even greater. Sunday school songs will rise up and accuse her of not being a sunbeam for Jesus: '*J-O-Y! J-O-Y!* Surely this must mean/Jesus first, Yourself last/and Others in between!' (to the tune of 'Jingle Bells', all you sad atheists out there). She will be feeling overlooked, overshadowed, over-worked, overweight and overexposed to the public eye.

That's the extreme. Most of us manage to avoid it a fair proportion of the time. We all have our favourite strategies for coping. If your husband is lionised the whole time, you need them. For heaven's sake, he is given a pulpit and positively encouraged to pontifi-cate from it. He is there for people at life's crisis points, and he knows the answers to life's Big Questions.

The chief coping mechanism is that staple of the Lonely Hearts column, the GSOH. I'm afraid it's true — here in the vicarage we snigger at our parishioners. We snigger at their malapropisms ('You're the first religious person I've met who isn't just out to pervert me'). We snigger at their accidental Spooner-isms while reading the Lesson ('They shall mount up on ings like weagles'). We snigger at typos on the service sheet ('Crown him with many crows, the Lamb upon the throne', 'Get thee behind me, Stan!'). What's more, we encourage our children to do the same. This rebounds upon our foolish heads, as children are so much worse at controlling their hysterics during solemn services, and they set you off again just as you were starting to get a grip. They say things like 'NO ONE expects the Spanish Inquisition!' when they catch sight of somebody in a red cassock, or in the case of my younger son, they draw eerily accurate caricatures of eminent church-men.

There is a formula for calculating the likelihood of disgracing yourself in church: unseemly mirth is directly proportional to the solemnity of the occasion. So things have predictably taken a turn for the worse since our move to the cathedral. (The most recent incident was triggered by a verse in Psalm 147: 'Neither doth he delight in any man's legs.') When you are supposed to be on your best behaviour it's amazing how many inappropriate thoughts occur to you. Even in the twenty-first century there is a vestigial expectation that clergy and their families will conduct themselves with decorum. This is probably why I am endlessly amused by those things I *think* of saying, but never actually do. My mum mentioned once that Pete and I both say 'Right!' and 'Good!' all the time (optimistically, perhaps — as though by repeating the words often enough, we can galvanise life into becoming both those things). We decided that there were worse expressions we might routinely be using, and for a while we experimented (in the privacy of the vicarage) with alternatives. 'Dickhead! — I'm off to my meeting, now.' 'Are you, darling? Bollocks!'

Sometimes it seems to me that my life is littered with tempting occasions for misbehaving. Oh, the parishioners I haven't slapped, the bishops I haven't goosed! The deanery Christmas parties where I have not passed out drunk! Once in a while someone will lay a hand on my arm and say very earnestly, 'He's ever so nice, your Pete, isn't he?' How to respond, how to respond? 'Actually, he's a bit of a pig.' Or, 'Nice?! See this bruise?' I normally agree and say I quite like him myself. Sometimes people tell me he's very clever, he's got a doctorate. I'VE GOT A BLOODY DOCTORATE AS WELL AND I GOT MINE BEFORE HE DID!

I never say that, partly because I am ever so nice too, but mostly because I find it hilarious when people confide this information, as though I might not have heard about it yet. 'Never! You know, I *thought* he was acting a bit funny, poncing about the vestry in that Little Red Riding Hood outfit!' If I felt insecure or overshadowed, it would be a different matter; one of grim seriousness.[1] There are times when this is the case. Usually it's fleeting. We all have days when we feel fat and useless. I rang a friend once and said, 'I feel fat and useless.' 'You're not *fat!*' she snorted. After a pause she added, 'You are useless, mind you.' Is there a woman anywhere who wouldn't prefer it that way round?

At other times the problem is more chronic. When I was pregnant with my second son and my brain had gone AWOL, I decided to pamper my ego by admiring my degree certificates. This was smug and elitist, so naturally I felt very guilty about all those people who have no recourse to this kind of academic bolstering. But stuff 'em anyway. Unfortunately, I had to ferret past no fewer

---

[1] My robust sense of self-worth doesn't stop me punching the air in triumph on those rare occasions when my husband is greeted with the words, 'Ah, you must be Mr Fox!' Fox is only a pen name, so that I can go deep undercover around the parish.

than six degree certificates belonging to my husband. *Six!* Fair enough, some of them were those spurious no-work-involved Oxbridge so-called MAs. But all the same.

This brought me up sharp and reminded me of my maxim about divvying up the turf in a relationship. If, like me, you are a premier league bad loser, you need to pick a partner whose strengths *complement*, rather than rival your own, because you are never too old to bash the board over if you are losing. Which is perhaps why we learned early on in our marriage how to play collaborative Scrabble. I shoved the degree certificates back in the drawer and stomped off to make a lemon meringue pie.

I'm sure it doesn't take much imagination to see what role judo might play in the life of a grumpy vicar's wife who spends a lot of her time reining in the urge to do something outrageous. At its simplest, judo *is* an outrageous thing to do. 'It satisfies my longings as nothing else can do!' as the hymn puts it.[1] Yes, judo satisfies. If once or twice a week I get to be violent, it's easier to be nice the rest of the time.

---

[1] The hymn is talking about something slightly different, but I'm taking the gamble that most of my readers won't know.

Make no mistake, being nice is important. I would like to go on record as saying that I think niceness is an underrated virtue nowadays. It is good to be nice to people. Whenever we are faced with the choice between smiling and giving someone a Chinese burn, we should smile every time. The world will be a better place.

Do you sense a 'However' approaching? However. There is a price tag attached to being relentlessly nice. Sometimes you feel as if you are about to explode. Or you start to feel like a hypocrite, as though part of your psyche has peeled off to form a separate identity, hidden from the unsuspecting parish. My eyes in the mirror turn bloodshot. Hairs sprout from the palms of my hands. Help! I've turned into a Were-vicar's-wife! When the moon is full I roam the streets howling for blood. I used to fantasise about installing a soundproof padded cell in the vicarage, so I could shut myself in for five minutes before the Bible Study group arrived and roar and curse and fling myself about gnashing my teeth, then emerge calm and smiling to make the coffee.

Some of you may well be wondering why I don't just let it all hang out. Why can't I just be 'real'? What's wrong with being bad-tempered and showing it? This is a very good

111

point. The difficulty lies in my being a semi-public figure. It's not about pretending to be perfect (although this is an easy trap to fall into). It's about not wanting to become the parish soap opera. I wish this were more straightforward. When bad things happen to me, people are concerned. I would be for them if they were facing a crisis. I know they wish me well — of course they do — but sometimes I just want to shout, *Go away!* It's probably the numbers involved. The nature of my husband's job means that we have a wider pool of well-wishers than most normal people do. But how can I grumble about that? Shouldn't I be grateful? Guilt, guilt.

These days I don't need a padded cell. I have a dojo. And I don't need to fling myself about now I can fling grown men instead. It is to the subject of flinging grown men about that we now turn.

★   ★   ★

In official contests, whether at local level or at the Olympics, men and women fight separately. However, there are many more male judo players than female in the UK, so if women want a range of opponents to practise against, they are probably going to end up fighting the blokes in their club at some point. From the woman's perspective, this is a good thing. If you spend your time fighting men, your game will improve. When you are next up against another woman, you will make mincemeat of her. That's the theory, anyhow. The flaw in this cunning plan is that the other woman has probably been doing exactly the same.

But how does it look from the male perspective? When we are pairing up to practise, are they looking at me and thinking, Oh no, who gets to be with Useless today? Occasionally, another even less welcome thought occurs to me: what if they are looking forward to rolling around on the mat with me and burying their sweaty face in my bosom under the flimsy pretext of pinning me down? In short, what if they enjoy it? Enjoy in a way that is an affront to the Spirit of Judo, I mean.

I genuinely can't tell whether I am flattering myself to think they do, or naive to think they don't. So I asked a member of the male sex for his opinion. He stared at me pityingly and said, 'Catherine, this is a no-brainer. They are *men*.' Unsatisfied with this reply, I asked my husband, who is, after all, an ordained minister in the Church of England, and likely to have a more elevated insight. 'What's not to enjoy?' was his wondering response.

Both these pathetic, puerile comments came from men who don't do judo, so I dismiss them out of hand. What do *they* know? It's not like that when you're on the mat. Honestly, we never think about that kind of thing. Speaking for myself, I definitely banish the notion far, *far* from my mind when I am flat on my back with my legs wrapped round a man's waist. All I am thinking is how to put an armlock on him without getting myself strangled. It's all about being professional. In a different setting — the back seat of a car, a hotel bedroom — the kind of sweaty limb-entanglement that occurs in judo would be unambiguously carnal. But context is everything. Think about being on a crowded Tube train. Just because your groin is pressed against another person's buttocks doesn't mean you automatically *enjoy* it. You mentally disengage, you dissociate yourself from what's happening. You start, rather urgently perhaps, to assemble your all-time greatest fantasy football team. Or consider massage: we all take it for granted that while massage is physical — indeed sensuous — it is not therefore sexual. Well, women take it for granted. Men perhaps have difficulty here. 'Reggie? Could you give me a back massage, darling? [*Two nanoseconds later*] That's NOT my back!'

Oh dear, oh dear. This is the crux of the problem: the conflicting things men and women take for granted. One of the popular conundrums in Consciousness Studies is 'What is it like to be a bat?' Forget bats: what is it like to be a *man*? I will never know. All I can do is ask. For obvious reasons, I hesitate to ask any of my clubmates what's *really* going on in their heads during a groundwork session. How would one phrase the question, exactly? 'Is that a nunchuck in your *judogi*, or are you just pleased to see me?'

No, I think our motto must be: *Don't Go There*. So we will move on maturely and calmly, and not at all in a flustered way, to another aspect of training in a mixed club: the size/strength discrepancy between the sexes.

One of the manifestations of the Spirit of Judo is courtesy and consideration. If you are a higher grade, you do not use your superior skills to slaughter your opponent. Instead, you adapt your fighting so as to put yourself on their level. If the other player manages a good technique, you sportingly allow yourself to be thrown. You say, 'Well done!' and perhaps offer a tip on how they might improve. Naturally, if they happen to throw you when you aren't expecting it, you will want to raise your game a little in response. If you are the lower grade player, you will usually be able to tell when you've snuck one past your opponent. The clue will be in the way they get to their feet, narrow their eyes and proceed to bury you repeatedly in the mat.

Broadly speaking, men who are fighting women will need to exercise restraint. They will usually be heavier and stronger than their female counterparts, so a macho bull-in-a-china-shop approach may result in broken bones. This is unpleasant for both parties; for the man because he will feel like a brute and a bully, and for the woman because she may never walk unaided again. In fact, if you are a tiny, birdlike blonde, you may want to think twice about fighting large men at all — although they will be very keen to take you on, for the exact reasons I have just stoutly denied. This is not to say that there is no such thing as a good small player; but if you pit a tiny player against a giant, the tiny player's techniques will have to be red hot and faster than the eye can see. This is the reason for weight categories at contests. Without them it just isn't a fair fight.

When I fight men, it is hardly ever a fair fight. This doesn't bother me. See how far I have travelled since I was eleven years old and eaten up with testosterone envy? These days

I'm reconciled to it. In a lot of ways I find fighting men less complicated than fighting women. I need have no compunction against an experienced male opponent. He's always going to beat me unless his guard is down or my timing is spot on (or he is utterly wet and a weed). I am unlikely to hurt him, except maybe with a badly executed *tomoe-nage*, a sacrifice throw that requires a foot placed squarely in the stomach. As you can imagine, this technique can go wrong in a way which makes women smirk and men wince.[1]

So when I'm fighting men I don't have to worry. Worrying will be the man's job. He will need to defend himself, and the honour of the male sex, by not getting himself ignominiously thrown; yet at the same time he will have to attack sufficiently often and hard enough not to come across as condescending and patronising. Basically, he will have to display that winning Mills & Boon combination of machismo and gentleness. Poor

---

[1] Kano describes the proper treatment (called *kogan-katsu*) for a man whose testicles have been kicked up into his pelvis. 'Put your arms under the [seated] patient's armpits from behind and clasp your hands together. Lift him up a bit and then let him drop. Repeat as necessary. Alternatively, lightly kick him in the lower back with the ball of your foot.'

sucker. The good news from his point of view is that this will be helpful in the wider world. Gentlemen, forget this New Man nonsense. The considerate bit of rough is a highly sought-after commodity. Or so I think, after some bloke hauls me effortlessly to my feet again after throwing me. The dojo is one of the few places where a big lass gets to feel petite.

When I fight women, my caring side sometimes overwhelms my killer instinct. Fights between women players in our club tend to be punctuated by expressions of concern: 'Are you OK?' 'Sorry, did I pull your hair?' My need to win is compromised by the impulse towards cooperation. Unfortunately, I tend to take this with me to gradings. I can't tap into that pure unadulterated aggression I know is there, and which is released when I am fighting men. Naturally, I want to win at gradings, but I feel a bit bad about beating people. Not *quite* as bad as I feel if they beat me, if I'm honest, and it is this that keeps me going.

Maybe this is more to do with being a handwringing middle-class clergy wife and mother-of-two than with being female. There are plenty of focused, ruthless women players out there. I would guess, though, that they are either a lot younger than I am and not tenderised by motherhood, or else they've been taking part in competitive sport since school and know how to compartmentalise. They are able to leave their emotional baggage at the side of the mat along with their trainers and electrolyte sports drinks.

It's the samurai spirit that I lack. If you trace the judo family tree way back, you will eventually encounter samurai warriors. Until recently, I had only the haziest notion of who the samurai were. Fortunately, my friend Richard, who used to live in Tokyo, sent me a copy of *Hagakure: The Book of the Samurai*, by the eighteenth-century master, Yamamoto Tsunetomo. I had not read far — in fact, only half a page — when I came upon this cogent summary: 'The Way of the Samurai is found in death.' That explains a lot, I thought.

It lies beyond the scope of this study (as we academics say when we don't really understand something and, frankly, can't be bothered to try) to explore the Samurai Way in any depth. Suffice it to say that the samurai were the elite warrior caste of Japan between the eleventh and nineteenth centuries. They knew more nasty ways to maim and kill people than you could shake a stick at. They famously had a nasty way of killing themselves as well: *seppuku*, better known to us in the West as *hara-kiri* (though this is vulgar slang). 'When it comes to either/or, there is only the quick choice of death. It is not particularly difficult' — just a simple matter of disembowelling yourself in a ceremonial manner with a sharp knife, while a good buddy, acting as ceremonial assistant (or *kaishaku*), stands by to behead you after you've done the deed.

When Tsunetomo was writing his book, the glory days of the samurai were already past. He had been prevented by law from committing *seppuku* after his master's death, and had retired instead to become a Buddhist monk. His writings have something of an ichabod feel to them:

> Thus I knew that men's spirit had weakened and that they had become the same as women, and the end of the world had come . . . When looking at the men of today with this in mind, those who could be thought to have a woman's pulse are many indeed, and those who seem like real men few . . . That there are few men who are able to cut well in beheadings is further proof that men's courage has waned.

It is very difficult for an English clergy wife in the twenty-first century to enter into the thought processes of the samurai. I have less difficulty imagining I'm a bat. From my perspective, the samurai world is an alien and frightening place: one where it was better to slit your stomach open than live in dishonour; where acting before thinking was commended; where single-minded, blind obedience to your master was the highest possible goal. Hanging upside down in a cave and eating moths is a breeze compared with this. Separated as I am from the warrior caste geographically, historically and culturally, what am I to make of the following?

In the judgment of the elders, a samurai's obstinacy should be excessive. A thing done with moderation may later be judged to be insufficient. I have heard that when one thinks he has gone too far, he will not have erred. This sort of rule should not be forgotten.

Tsunetomo elaborates on this theme by offering his analysis of how a drunken brawl on board ship ought to have been dealt with:

Now, first of all, it was an insufficiency on the master's part not to have reproved and pacified the drunken page while they were on board the boat. Furthermore, even though the page had acted unreasonably, after he had been struck on the head there was no reason for apology. The master should have approached the sailor and the drunken page in an apologetic manner and cut them both down. Certainly he was a spiritless master.

I really can't get a handle on this.[1] Short of going and living in Japan, immersing myself in its language, culture and history, and training five nights a week at the Kodokan, I fear I never will. Sadly, it lies beyond the scope of my life to do any of these things. Maybe in the next life? Will there be judo in heaven?[2]

To what extent is judo a true descendant of the Samurai Way? Samurai techniques were originally top secret, and handed on only to members of the warrior caste. 'But with the

---

[1] Although I warm to his comment, 'Personally, I like to sleep. And I intend to appropriately confine myself more and more to my living quarters and pass my life away sleeping.'

[2] I once asked Keith this, and he laughed bitterly and said, 'If there is, I hope it's easier than it is here.' Certainly he is a spiritless sensei! He has a woman's pulse and I should have cut him down. Apologetically, of course.

passing away of the old order of things together with the Shogun,' Uyenishi tells us in his introduction to *The Text-Book of Ju-Jutsu*, 'the Samurai ceased to be a caste apart and gave to their country not only their own priceless services, but also all their great store of knowledge in the science of physical well-being and self-defence.'

It was this great store of knowledge that Kano ransacked and codified and offered to the world as judo — rejecting the more evil and dangerous techniques, I am heartily glad to say. As Uyenishi claims, 'So much care has been devoted to the preservation of the purely sporting element of Ju-jutsu, that I venture to claim among its other virtues that of being the least dangerous to life and limb of any sport or contest in existence.' Well, I'm not sure how Uyenishi played ping-pong or chess, but let's not argue. I feel able to endorse the statement conservatively, in the sense that considering how violent judo can be, I'm amazed how few injuries there are.

It is not just judo's techniques that are inherited from the samurai. The scoring system also smacks of the Samurai Way. Even though nobody chops your head off, judo is a sudden-death business. If you lose to a full score (*ippon*), that's it. No second chance, no comeback. A bout can be over in two seconds. It would be like playing football with the Golden Goal rule in operation from kick-off. Kano was not happy with this, and always felt that a greater stress should be put upon training by *kata* (learning by a series of structured moves) than on *randori*. In Kano's mind, the heart of judo was cooperation. '*Ji ta kyo ei*' — 'By helping yourself, everybody benefits.' The second half of this maxim is easily forgotten in the heat of contest after it has travelled halfway round the globe and been translated into English. Instead of Kano's measured wisdom we get that egregious Western watchword, 'Look after number one.' Or 'God helps those who help themselves.' Just for the record, that phrase does not occur anywhere in the Bible.

Your First Grading

What the Bible does promise is that those who call upon the name of the Lord will be saved. This is a good verse to hang onto when you are approaching your first grading. These are generally held at large venues and people will travel from all over the area, or even the length of the country, to compete for their next belt. You will generally have at least two contests against people who are roughly your weight and ability.

By the time you are ready to have a go at your orange belt, you will have done your orange-belt theory and got it signed up in your licence book. You will be called onto a mat to line up with all the other novices. Some will still be wearing white belts, but most will be 9th kyu yellow belts. According to my trusty handbook, 'Kyu means a senior student of 16 years or over who has attained a grade denoted by a coloured belt.' For some reason, kyu grades start at 9 and go down until you are a 1st kyu brown belt, fighting for your 1st dan black belt. At this point it switches: dan grades go *up*. I have no idea why, and it's confusing.[1] Even people who have been doing judo for a long time rarely know instinctively that 4th kyu is blue belt, for example. They have to stop and work it out. It's a bit like the new system of school years. What's year 9? Hang on — that must be 3rd form in old money.

To make things even harder, there are two

---

[1] Just for fun, junior, or '*mon*' grades, also go up rather than down. A junior brown belt would be a 16th *mon*, or 17th, or indeed 18th — there are three levels per belt for juniors. These are signified by little stripes on the end of the belt. I hope this makes things a bit clearer.

kyu grades for each colour of belt, so you might either get bottom or top orange at your first grading, depending on how well you fight. The difference between top and bottom of the same colour is only an issue when you are lining up to bow before the start of a session. You always line up in strict grade order, highest grade on the right, facing the coaches and dan grades. I sometimes sense that in the masculine mind, a male 1st kyu ranks higher than a female 1st kyu,[1] so now and then I plant myself at the top and refuse to budge. This is against the Spirit of Judo, where humility is a cherished virtue. It's also against the spirit of Christianity, come to think of it, where the first shall be last. However, it is not against the spirit of feminism, so up yours, mate.

It is an exciting moment when you get the first coloured belt you have actually fought for. Belts will probably be on sale at the grading, but you can also buy them at sports shops. It feels pretty cool to walk in and ask for a judo brown belt, even if you can tell the assistants are thinking it's for your son. On a

---

[1] My coach Debbie endorses this impression. I asked her if some men underestimated her ability because she's a woman. They do, apparently, and it does her head in.

126

very bad day, I fear they are thinking grandson.

Belts come in different lengths, and if you are sensible you won't leave this to chance. The only trouble is, they are measured in centimetres, and who over the age of twenty knows their waist measurement in centimetres? If the truth be told, many of us don't even know our waist measurement in inches, since we are optimistically imagining it is the same as it was fifteen years ago and that clothes manufacturers must all be conspiring to save fabric by making waistbands smaller. So what does length matter? Well, my blue belt would have gone round me three times it was so long. The ends dangled almost to my knees. I expect I should have bitten it in half, or asked a karate player to chop some off. They probably do that all the time when they've run out of breeze blocks.

Some players, generally big blokes, wear incredibly short belts that only just tie up. This could either be for tactical reasons, to present the opponent with fewer opportunities, or because it looks macho. Secretly, I think it's because they are FAT, but with experience comes wisdom. I know to keep this opinion to myself.

Here's a little laundry tip: don't wash your new belt with your kit. Judo belts are not colour fast, and you will end up with an orange *judogi*. Laundry mishaps will always be ridiculed in the dojo, so watch out, particularly, for that stray red sock in the white load. It takes a confident player to pull off the pink kit look.

Kano notes that 'Personal hygiene is also important. Students should be clean and keep their fingernails and toenails short to avoid injuring others. The *judogi* should be washed regularly and any tears mended promptly.' I definitely agree with regular kit washing. (Washing? What for? Just stick it on the radiator, love.) There is a temptation to put off those needlework repairs. A stitch in time may save nine, but a ripped *gi* makes you look well-hard. It's a sort of testosterone marker, like a baboon's backside, or a turkey wattle. This is illogical, when you stop to think about it. All it really says is that you've been up against a well hard opponent, or that your kit is ancient. But logic doesn't feature prominently in the dojo. A torn sleeve, like a black eye, is always going to be a badge of honour. Anyway, if you persist in wearing it, maybe some woman in the club will crack and say, 'Oh, give it to me for heaven's sake and I'll mend it for you!'

Torn jackets can be used strategically. Keith tells of an occasion when someone turned up to a contest wearing one, knowing he'd be told to change. He then took off his torn jacket by ripping it clean in half before the assembled crowd. All his opponents naturally thought, Bloody hell! This bloke rips *gis* with his bare hands! — not realising that a determined toddler could probably have done the same.

Another laundry tip: lifting bloodstains from white cotton. Don't bung it in a hot wash, as this will set the stain permanently. Soak it in cold water first, or spray it with a stain remover. The likely places for blood are the lapels and sleeves (from your opponent's bloody knuckles), or inside the sleeves (from your own raw elbows), or all down the front (nose-bleed). Gallons of gore and buckets of blood! as my mother used to say lugubriously. I forget why. Grazed knees, probably. We don't object to a bit of blood down at the dojo.

Unless it's menstrual blood, of course. *That* would be monumentally embarrassing and we never talk about such things. Women may allude to the time of the month among themselves, rolling their eyes and saying, 'Tell me about it!' (meaning, 'Actually, don't'). Too much information, as the young people say. Except young people seem much cooler about menstruation than women of my age and older. I was moaning about periods with a teenage girl once while we got changed. How come you can't get red judo kits? That would be handy, we thought. However, she thought leaking on the mat was far less embarrassing than having your trousers rip to reveal you were in need of a bikini wax. We stared at one another in mutual incomprehension.

It's a generation gap thing. My very kind husband will occasionally buy sanitary items for me if he knows exactly what he is looking for. Browsing is out. He gets flustered by wings and absorbency levels. Our older son thinks this is hilarious. Like women don't have periods, durr! Maybe this is because he has never stood, as my husband has, at a supermarket checkout, and overheard a hissed exchange from an old couple behind him. 'Did you see *that*?!' 'Yes! Very strange! VERY STRANGE!' Never go shopping in a dog collar. And if you do, never pay with loads of loose change. People will think you've been dipping into the collection plate.

In previous eras, menstruation was an insurmountable barrier to strenuous exercise. Or a jolly good excuse, if my memories of grammar-school swimming lessons are anything to go by. There was a trio of hardened refusniks in my class who were 'on' three weeks out of four. Since then we have been blessed with huge advances in sanitary technology. We are promised breatheability and freshness. Thinnest ever! Ultra absorbent! But best of all, they offer us *confidence*.

If only confidence could be bought over the counter. Unfortunately, confidence in judo can only be acquired through experience, and experience usually involves hitting the ground very hard. Repeatedly. This is why I like groundwork. 'He that is down need fear no fall,' as the hymn puts it.

Judo is divided into two types of fighting — standing work (*tachi-waza*) and groundwork (*ne-waza*). It's true that Kano also includes *atemi-waza*, striking techniques. But as he says these are only practised in *kata* (formal demonstration), and '*never in randori*', for all practical purposes, they play no part in judo. Groundwork is much nicer because you won't be dropped on your head from a great height, and you get to strangle people. That's just a personal opinion. Many people prefer *tachi-waza*. You are allowed to strangle people in standing work, but there is a chance that a) you will get thrown while you are attempting it and b) the ref won't spot what you are trying to do, and will penalise you for 'passivity'.

For safety reasons, you are not permitted to throw someone while you are strangling them. The same applies to armlocks. Unlike other martial arts, judo is not about breaking bones and killing people. If you think this makes it a sissy sport, you have much to learn, my young grasshopper. The constraints make it less sissy, if anything, as you can follow through fully with all your techniques, rather than having to pull out of them. Judo is *the* total full-body contact sport. It's like rugby, only without all that tedious running around. When you apply your strangles and joint locks, it is up to the other person to submit if their arm is about to break or their eyeballs pop out.

In a contest you always start off with standing work, but you frequently end up on the mat after being thrown, or (in my case) after you have tripped yourself up. If nothing much is happening down there, the ref will get bored and make you stand up again. Should you feel that the other person is dominating you on the ground, you are well advised to try and stagger back to your feet even if they are still clamped onto you like a limpet. Again, the ref will then restart the bout with both players standing.

At club level it is common to concentrate on standing work or groundwork separately, rather than swapping back and forth between the two. Again, this is for safety reasons. You don't want people on the ground while others are rampaging around the mat doing standing work, in case someone gets thrown on top of another player. You have to keep an ear cocked the whole time for the coach shouting '*Matte!*',[1] which is what will happen if he or she sees an accident about to happen.

Groundwork has three components — hold-downs (*osae-komi-waza*), strangles (*shime-waza*) and joint techniques (*kansetsu-waza*). In judo, joint techniques are restricted to arm (more precisely, elbow) locks. This can be tough on players who have done some ju-jitsu, as they instinctively resort to wrist and neck locks in the heat of the moment. This will result in disqualification at contests, or, at club level, in everyone shouting annoyingly, 'You can't do that!'

To summarise: 'In grappling the opponent is held, his joints are locked or his limbs twisted and bent, or he can be strangled.' With that generous permission from our revered founder — enjoy!

Hold-down techniques do tend to favour the heftier player, so fatties, permit yourselves a sly smile. Technique is important, of course, but there's nothing like a bit of weight to

---

[1] I stated earlier that '*matte*' means 'stop'. This is what my BJA handbook says, and how most people understand the word. I learned last week that it actually means 'wait!'. The word for stop is '*yame*'.

reinforce it. I'd hesitate to say that *osae-komi-waza* can be reduced to 'lying on top of someone and squashing them', but this is a helpful starting point for the novice trying to visualise it. Basically you are attempting to keep your opponent's shoulders pinned to the mat for a certain length of time. There many ways of doing this, and along with each new hold-down you master, you should also be taught the various escapes. But trust me, once your opponent has settled into a hold, it is bloody hard to get out.

When the ref spots a proper hold, he or she will call '*Osae-komi!*' and the clock will start. The player applying the technique then hangs on for dear life while their opponent busts a gut trying to escape before time is up. This is twenty-five seconds for an *ippon*. It will feel like five minutes if you are doing the pinning down and five seconds if you are trying to escape. If the pinner-down[1] already has a score to their credit, the time will be correspondingly shorter. If you do manage to escape, or to trap the other player's leg above the knee between your own, the ref will shout

---

[1] The official term for someone executing a technique is '*tori*'. The person on the receiving end is called '*uke*'.

134

'*Toketa!*' (hold broken).[1]

Kesa-gatame is one of the first holds you learn, and remains a firm favourite in most players' repertoire. It wins many contests. The English translation is 'scarf hold' (*kesa* being the sash of a Buddhist monk) because you immobilise your opponent with an arm round the neck. The unfortunate *uke* will be flat on his or her back, and you will be crushing them, ribcage to ribcage, sitting right beside them with your legs spread 'to create a firm base', as my BJA guide advises, an arm wrapped round their neck under their head (like a scarf — always supposing the scarf in question has been possessed by the evil spirit of a boa constrictor). One of their arms should be clamped under your other armpit. I know, hard to picture, isn't it? But believe me, it works. A small person can pin down a much larger person with this technique if they know what they are doing. As your opponent attempts to escape, you must adjust your position to prevent them. Funnily enough, you sometimes need to

---

[1] Or so my handbook tells me. For all I know, it could mean 'You have brought shame on your family and must now disembowel yourself!' This is the problem with not speaking any Japanese.

relax into it and lie on them like a dead weight. If you brace yourself rigid, they may find it easier to bridge and roll you off.

I once lost two fights at a grading when I was pinned down with *kesa-gatame*. On the second occasion I managed to squirm right round until I was practically lying on my stomach, but as one shoulder was still on the mat, the hold was still on. The following day I could barely move. I'd pulled all my intercostals.[1] Once someone has settled into *kesa-gatame*, something in me gives up and dies. *Well, I'll never get out of this*, says my brain in glum resignation.

This kind of fatalism must be resisted at all costs. You have to remember how long that twenty-five seconds will be feeling to the other player. Go berserk, attempt all your escapes, then try them again. I can think of many occasions when I've been pinning someone who has practically got out, only for them to slump into despair at the crucial

---

[1] These are the muscles between your ribs. I remember the name by thinking of them as the 'Pentecostal muscles', the ones you might strain by waving your arms about too enthusiastically during a charismatic revival.

moment. I tell them afterwards, 'You were nearly out then, you know.' 'Well, that's not what it felt like!' they reply.

I try hard to remember this, but when I hear the ref say, '*Osae-komi!*', that glum old voice still goes, *Oh bugger, that's it*. It reminds me of doing high jump at school, when you look at the bar and suddenly think, *I'll never get over that*. Even if it's only one centimetre higher than last time, once you've thought this, you're stuffed.

This happens to me, sometimes, if I am up against a very big or scary-looking opponent. I just *know* they are going to beat me. Naturally, this is a self-fulfilling prophecy. I wish I could get over this — with mental preparation, perhaps. I asked one of the senior grade men at my club for advice, and he said, 'What I do is imagine my opponent has just killed every member of my family. Then I imagine that I am going to get my revenge and kill *him*.' I didn't find this particularly helpful. If someone has just wiped out my entire family, the chances are they are a dangerous psychopath, and the best plan is to run. Neither can I simply repeat the mantra *I'm going to win!* because I'm not that good at lying to myself. Well, not outright whoppers, at any rate. Little white ones now and then, such as 'I may have sixty-seven pairs of shoes, but I really *need* these silver stilettos'.

I realise that what I ought to do is call upon past experience of fights where appearances have been deceptive. This was true when I was fighting for my top blue belt. My first bout was against a much shorter opponent. She was short, but she was stocky, and boy, was she tough. She eventually won, and as we shook hands and bowed off I could see stars. My fingers couldn't grip, my arms and legs were trembling and my lungs felt about to implode. My next opponent had exactly the same build. Oh bloody hell, not *again*! I thought. But the instant I took hold of her and yanked, I felt the difference. She was soft where the other woman was hard. Hah! Gotcha! I threw her over and pinned her down (*yoko-shiho-gatame* — side four-quarters hold), and it was all over in a flash.

See? You never can tell. It just might be all right.

If only I could learn from this. As I waited miserably for the start of my last grading I found myself thinking, How come being a Christian makes no difference at all? You'd think that all those years of prayer would help, wouldn't you? The real bummer about the life of faith is that rescue isn't guaranteed. I suppose the clue is in the cross.[1] Even when help comes, it frequently turns out to be help *through* rather than *out of* the circumstances. 'Lead us not into temptation' always sounds like a plea for help when our hand hovers over the Quality Street tin. Ooh, I mustn't, I mustn't! A better translation of the Greek would be 'Do not bring us to the time of trial'. What the Lord's Prayer is actually talking about is the acute testing that all human beings dread, those times when the last thing you want is the strength to endure. Stuff that — get me out of here!

What happened to the peace that passes all understanding? I whimper inside, while I wait for my bout to be called. But somehow I manage to carry on anyhow. Not particularly nobly, or courageously, or even very well, but I do still manage to do it. I'm beginning to see how judo is a big and flexible metaphor for my life. If I can do it here in the dojo, I can do it elsewhere. I can face things and see

---

[1] I take this for granted, but my husband met someone recently who'd watched the whole of Mel Gibson's *The Passion of the Christ*, without knowing how the story ended. She'd been assuming it was a kind of first-century *Die Hard*, and that at the eleventh hour, Jesus would escape.

things through to the end. Everything passes. Sometimes you are *tori*, sometimes you're *uke*. That's the way it is in this life. As I tell my younger son when he is anxious about something and wishes he was braver: 'Being brave doesn't mean not being scared. It means doing something even though you are scared.'

Sometimes people tell me that Christianity is just a crutch. I think, yeah, that would be nice, wouldn't it?

Diary

20 June 2005
Haven't been writing this diary for a while. I couldn't face it. So there's a lot of catching up. If I leave it any longer it will fade — which is what I want. But it would also be lost.

Hot day, though cooler than yesterday. We had a monsoon as we went to church in the evening. I stood in the doorway watching. Spray billowing up like smoke; all the rooftops and streets and parked cars seemed to be on fire. Thunder was racketing overhead. Hailstones the size of marbles came clattering down. People were running past screaming with laughter to start with, though later they were walking, resigned and soaked to the skin.

I've started running a longer route home from school now, to try and up my fitness levels. I now do just under three miles, which takes me twenty-seven minutes. I hate it. I distract myself on hills by casting my mind back to New Zealand. Nothing in Walsall counts as steep by Wellington standards. My other strategy is to pray for people. It helps me, and sometimes it may help them. You can't tell with prayer whether things would have turned out that way if you'd never bothered to ask.

The three-mile run started when I came back from teaching another writing course in Devon. Pete picked me up from Walsall station. After listening to me for a while, he said he had some sad news to tell me. Debbie had phoned to say that a group of lads from the club had been to Nottingham to celebrate someone's stag night, and a speeding car had hit Neil. He was killed instantly.

It takes the mind a while to catch up. At first your brain is telling you the information is small, insignificant. You are half laughing in disbelief: 'What? No! You mean — ?' You want to say, 'He can't be, I only saw him last week! I was fighting him and he said — ' But even as you are protesting, disbelief gives way, collapses like a tall building falling in on itself. You want to scream NO!

That's why I went on a long run with Pete. We'd been planning this for a while, and he said, 'You may not feel like it, now.' But I thought, Yes I do. It was partly because I knew I'd only sit at home and howl otherwise, and the boys would try to comfort me, and they've had enough of that this last year. It was partly the thought of Neil, and how he'd been badgering me the previous Saturday to enter contests and go along to the training nights at the new judo centre, and telling me I'd got no excuse. He said, 'You'll get your line up,' and I said, 'No I won't,' and he said, 'Yes you will, you'll do well. Yow'm strong, I'm going to have to start throwing you now.'

When we'd finished the run, I lay on our front lawn looking up at the sky through the sycamore leaves, watching the swallows and house martins wheeling in the perfect blue.

I had a strong image of him watching us the following Saturday, at the points when we broke off from training and sat hopelessly on the mat and talked about him, about how awful it was for us all, but mostly for those closest to him, and for those who saw him die. I could picture him rolling his eyes and saying, 'Well, get on with it!'

His funeral was last Friday. The church in Wednesbury was packed. So many people I only ever see in white all dressed in black. Pete and I were in the crowd who arrived too late for a seat and had to stand in the entrance lobby. The vicar said in her opening words, 'We won't allow the circumstances of his death to cheat us out of the chance of celebrating his life.' I think she struck the right note. She read us a letter from his young son. His Major — Neil had been in the TA — made us laugh with

143

anecdotes from his army career. We sang 'There is a Green Hill Far Away' and 'Give me Joy in my Heart', which apparently was Neil's favourite. His coffin was carried out by members of his squadron to 'We are the Champions.' Yeah, we probably will all go on fighting until the end. But if the Gospel means anything at all, then the gates of glory will be flung open to losers as well.

27 June 2005

Sometimes you have to be careful what you wish for. I set off for a long run on Saturday morning, knowing I wasn't going to be able to get to judo, because our curate was being priested that afternoon. *I wish I didn't have to do this*, a little voice inside me moaned. I ploughed on. As I slogged up our road I saw a florist's van. *I wish someone would give me a bunch of flowers*, moaned the little voice. Shut up, I replied.

My mind resembles a badly edited stream-of-consciousness novel when I am running. What am I going to wear to Jenny's ordination? My new linen trousers? Shall I run the full three miles? No. But Neil would be disappointed in me. Good, this bit's down-hill, lengthen stride, that smells nice — honeysuckle, oh look, a lady with a dog, I'll let her go through the gate first.

My next thought was SHIT! Actually, that was my next word, as the dog leapt up and chomped my leg. I'm not sure who was more shocked and upset. The owner was crying, I was crying (only with shock, you understand) and we were both doing our best to put it right, in that cooperative way women have, out-apologising one another. Neither of us was making much sense as we headed back towards her house. She invited me in, but I said I only lived round the corner. We established that our house backs on to her mother's and that her mother probably had some of our cricket balls. We promised to stay in touch and I limped off.

For years now I've been reassuring my younger son that if a dog is with its owner and on a lead, then it's probably OK. He's been wary of dogs since he was chased by a couple of big boxers when he was three. Boxer dogs, that is. Little by little he's mastered his fear. We have a running joke when we are walking to school and meet people walking their dogs. I whisper, 'Don't worry, love, he won't hurt you!' and my son whispers back, 'Well, he's never done *that* before!'

All dog owners say this. I get so fed up with this cheery reassurance and smirking at scared little boys, that I'm tempted to pre-empt it and call, 'Don't worry, he won't hurt it!' to the dog owner. Then when my son boots the dog as we pass, I'll say in shocked tones, 'Well, he's never done *that* before!'

In this instance the owner and I behaved impeccably. The dog has been put down, I haven't sued, *and* I got my bunch of flowers. This was most welcome. What was less welcome was the three-hour wait in A&E, even though I had a good book. It gave me plenty of time to people watch, though, and work out how the triage system operates. I think there are three categories: 1. Serious ('Stand aside, his testicles are all scalded!'); 2. Hopping/Limping (this appeared to be fairly evenly divided between sport and leisure injuries, the latter involving high heels and alcohol); and 3. Timewasters — sorry, *Minor* Injuries — into which category I insultingly fell. (There is also a fast-track Bad Parent category, for children who have downed a bottle of Calpol. I just happen to know this from somewhere. I forget where. Oh yes — personal experience.)

Eventually I was seen and my leg reassembled with Steri-Strips and a disappointingly small, ordinary plaster. Happily, it all looked a lot more spectacular when blood soaked through my cream linen trousers during the ordination service. I will know I'm a real grown-up when I am injured and I don't care if nobody at all ever knows about it.

All this means I will have to take a week off

training until the wound has healed. The timing isn't great, as the next grading is on 10 July. I was going to train so hard, and be the fittest and strongest I've ever been. The truth is, it probably wouldn't have made a scrap of difference. Instead I will fall back on my trusty plan B — denial. I'm afraid Neil would shake his head in disgust.

4

Green Belt

Onward, Christian soldiers!
　Marching as to war,
With the cross of Jesus
　Going on before.
Christ the royal master
　Leads against the foe;
Forward into battle,
　See, his banners go.

Hymn 50, 'Onward, Christian Soldiers'
in *With Cheerful Voice: Hymns for Children*

Fighting the Good Fight

There isn't much fighting talk in church nowadays. This is probably the result of decades of dominance in church structures and thought by liberal catholics (the seventies hand-wringing branch of the C of E). We are in the midst of a sea change in the Church of England of course, with evangelicals now in

148

ascendancy, but that hasn't yet played out fully throughout the whole of church life. Modern hymn books still veer towards inclusive language and nonviolence. There is a real squeamishness about war imagery. *Hymns Old & New, New Anglican Edition* has bowdlerised the old favourite 'Onward, Christian Soldiers, marching as to war.' Instead it offers 'Onward, Christian Pilgrims, Christ will be our light.' The introduction explains:

> We were concerned that the book should use positive and appropriate images, and decided that militarism and triumphalism were, therefore, not appropriate. We recognise that military imagery is used in the Bible, but history, including current events, shows only too clearly the misuse to which those images are open. All too often, in the Christian and other religions, texts advocating *spiritual* warfare are used to justify the self-serving ambitions behind temporal conflicts.

Well, ye-e-es. I see what they mean, but what about the times when martial imagery genuinely expresses what we are experiencing? When life really does feel like a battle, and you are under attack from all sides?

When we lived in Gateshead, the vicarage was on the edge of what was called 'an area of relative deprivation' (the PC way of saying 'rough'). Ours was the only detached house in an area made up of Victorian terracing and high-rise flats. You'd have to go about a mile before you found another detached house, and that was the vicarage of the neighbouring parish. We lived on the corner of the rugby field and most people assumed our house was an orphanage or old people's home, council offices, or just vaguely 'something to do with the rugby club'.

Our geographical position made the vicarage garden a tempting short cut for local children heading for the playing field. The strip of wasteland against our back fence was an excellent place for dens, or for experimenting with matches at the end of a long dry summer. Our front-garden wall was low and, being on the corner of two streets, it became the place for youngsters to congregate. And there was an electrical substation at the garden's end. It had a flat roof. Kids would climb on it and dare one another to jump into our garden.

When we arrived we were repeatedly warned about crime levels and advised to lock our doors and windows at all times and to keep the car in the garage at night. The first time we failed to do this our car was stolen and written off. (We'd had friends staying overnight, so we'd put their car in the garage instead. Being middle class, they apologised.) The vicarage had a burglar alarm like a war siren and I could never sleep unless we'd armed it.

During the course of the five years we spent on Tyneside, there were only a handful of occasions when anything bad actually happened. Unfortunately, there were a couple of incidents early on, and I never fully recovered. Even now, living on the Cathedral Close, if I hear rowdy voices in the night, a cold surge of adrenalin drenches me and for a second I'm rigid with terror. (Then I remember and think, Bloody choral scholars.) The worst occasion in Gateshead was one winter night when Pete was out and a gang of teenagers started rampaging round the garden hammering on windows and ringing the doorbell. Our older son was in his cot asleep and I was heavily pregnant. I sat on the stairs weeping, praying they'd go away, unable to decide whether dialling 999 was sensible, or if that would simply up the stakes and turn vicar-baiting into the latest game. Eventually, after smashing a window, they got bored and went away.

At moments like this 'Onward, Christian

Pilgrims' simply didn't work. My favourite hymn in Gateshead was 'Oft in Danger, Oft in Woe'. The second verse was a continual challenge to me:

> Onward, Christians, onward go,
> Join the war, and face the foe;
> Will ye flee in danger's hour?
> Know ye not your Captain's power?

The answer to the first question was, 'Given the chance, you bet!' Fleeing wasn't an option, however. I could see that there were two ways in which the situation might improve. Either the vandalism would stop, or I would toughen up. My mother, a good Christian woman, promised to pray for the youths who were causing me so much grief. I mentioned this to my sister Ruth. 'I'll pray they fall under a bus if you like,' she offered. The least supportive response was from a student from the nearby theological college, who was scandalised by my vision of razor wire with mains electricity running through it. I should be living out the Gospel by welcoming these marginalised youths into my home! But she was living in Durham and sending her children to the cathedral school, so I think, with hindsight, I am permitted to hunt her down and wallop her over the head with a copy of *Bias to the Poor*. At the time her criticism crushed me.

In the end I did toughen up a bit. One night I had a strange dream. I was crossing a farmyard and a flock of geese lowered their heads and charged, hissing. I tried to run, but tripped, and they were upon me, battering me with their wings. I screamed for help. Eventually it dawned on me that nobody was coming to rescue me. And the pecking didn't actually hurt much. Feeling queasy with each punch I landed, I began to beat them off. Finally I struggled back to my feet. When I woke I thought about the dream. It seemed charged with meaning, if only I could decipher it. Suddenly the phrase 'Wouldn't say boo to a goose' sprang to mind. I laughed out loud.

Learning to say boo to the geese in my garden was hard. Once, when Pete was predestined to be away for a week at the International Calvin Congress, I saw a group of children jumping off the flat roof into the garden. I forced myself to go out and confront them. 'I don't care if you play on the roof, but don't jump into the garden.' My older son was three at the time and simply roared, 'Get down! Get down!' 'The woman said we didn't have to,' they replied. 'She's not a woman, she's a LADY!' We went back into the house, and immediately several children jumped, so I had to go back out and confront them. 'Right! If you do that again there'll be BIG TROUBLE!' *Big trouble* — that is so pathetic, I castigated myself as I returned to the house. To my amazement it did the trick.

I learned to love Gateshead and its people. (Well, most of them.) The vandalism wasn't personal. I realised this when I saw the same gang of kids on a different roof in another bit of town. And when I stop to think about it, I did my share of rampaging round other people's gardens when I was a child. It would never have occurred to me there might be adults in the house terrified. Pete became a well-loved figure. He could park our car with impunity on the parish's most notorious estate. Everyone knew it was the vicar's car. The time he visited in a borrowed car, it was gone in twenty minutes. (He apologised to the owner.)

Living on the Cathedral Close is a bit like being in an idyllic village in the fifties with an enormous parish church. I love it. But a few weeks ago Pete and I found ourselves in a run-down part of Stoke-on-Trent on a rainy Friday, and just for a moment I missed Gateshead. I missed it the way I miss the north wind when I've been cooped up too long indoors. When you've lived in a place long enough, the oddest things make you homesick. I remember talking to a priest who had just moved from an inner urban parish. 'Did they used to smash your milk bottles? I kind of miss that,' he said wistfully.

We don't get much milk-bottle smashing here on the Close. In fact, there isn't much crime at all, though people get jolly cross if you say that, and immediately rattle off a long list of break-ins. Being burgled is always unpleasant, and I don't want to belittle the distress it causes, but the crime list would be more scary if the time scale were weeks, rather than years. The lack of time we devote to grumbling about the problem reveals its insignificance. Our energies are absorbed by the infinitely more heinous crime of people pinching our reserved parking spaces.

Personally, I have decided to be peaceable on this matter (and on its companion issue, the clogging up of the Close with 4×4s during the school run). 'I didn't sign up for peaceability!' says my husband, storming out to stick a shirty notice on yet another car parked on double yellows and blocking our access. This, like the use of militaristic imagery in hymns, is clearly an area in which Christians disagree. Which of us is right? I was pondering this when it occurred to me to ask the Bishop of Lichfield. His opinion would be worth having. Is he peaceable? Does he see himself as a soldier as well as a pilgrim? Is fighting talk acceptable in hymns? I went across the Close to ask him.

Of course it is. It is a metaphor. We need to understand the role of metaphorical language in our faith, 'Or there would only be sheep in heaven,' he pointed out. The problem comes when an image is treated literally, as with Bush's War on Terrorism. 'You can't literally have a war on terrorism. Wars are between armies. But Bush seems to think you can.'

I told him a bit about my experience in Gateshead, and the woman who had criticised me. 'And where was she living at the time?' he enquired. Exactly. Thank you, Bishop.

It turns out that Bishop Jonathan did a bit of judo himself as a child, although he can't really remember much of it. 'Except possibly how to fall.' He certainly didn't use any pin-downs or armlocks the time he apprehended a youth escaping through his main gates. Gosh! Bishop Makes Citizen's Arrest! I liked the sound of that. He explained that residents were being harassed by gangs of lads running amok in their gardens and stealing things. Catching and hanging on to one of the perpetrators seemed the right thing to do, 'Although I felt like a complete heel, because he was crying.' The police arrived promptly and the bishop got his secateurs back.

'And did that solve the crime problem on your side of the Close?' I asked.

'No.' He smiled benevolently. 'I think the razor wire did that.'

★   ★   ★

What Would Jesus Do? For those of you unfamiliar with this question (often abbreviated to WWJD), it is an evangelical catchphrase, designed to help us navigate our way though the ethical minefield of twenty-first-century life. WWJD crops up on wristbands and T-shirts, but also — in my opinion — on a wide range of less plausible merchandise. My younger son, for example, once had a WWJD yo-yo. The yo-yo was crap, so one possible answer might have been, 'Jesus would buy a better yo-yo.'

Now and then I encounter evangelicals who are much more fundamentalist and conservative than I am, and they look askance at judo because of its oriental non-Christian origins. WWJD? Why, Jesus would denounce judo as satanic! This is part of a package of beliefs which typically includes a hostility to hypnotherapy and yoga (opens the door to demon possession), to Harry Potter (promotes witchcraft), to woman priests and practising homosexuality (contradicts the Bible), and to black pudding (contains blood). I made the last one up, but technically, they *should* be opposed to eating meat with blood in, because the book of Acts says this is one of the bits of the Old Testament law that is binding on Gentiles. But apparently you can pick and choose what you believe. (Unless it's to do with the gay issue.)

I once gave a talk to a church group and exhorted them all to take up judo. They applauded politely, but the collective thought bubble over their heads clearly read, 'I'd rather have root canal fillings.' Afterwards a woman approached me and said, 'I thought we weren't supposed to approve of judo.' Here, in one sentence, is an example of the mindset that makes me feel like committing *seppuku* for being an evangelical, too. She knew next to nothing about judo, but was anxious about what she was 'supposed' to think. That's the Soundness Police at work — the evangelical version of the Spanish Inquisition. She had a vague impression that because judo has its origins in a Buddhist culture, it must automatically be tainted by the Devil. 'Judo is just a sport,' I told her. 'Doesn't it have a spiritual dimension?' she asked. I guffawed. 'Not the way we do it!' Certainly no more than rugby has a spiritual dimension because it was invented at a Christian public school.

It is true, as Kano points out, that the word *dojo* 'comes from a Buddhist term referring to the 'place of enlightenment'. Like a monastery, the dojo is a sacred place to which people come to perfect body and mind.' For someone worried that judo is the slippery slope to the occult, this is hardly reassuring. But just between you and me, a dojo in the West Midlands is not necessarily the same as a dojo in Tokyo. Oak Park Leisure Centre, Walsall Wood, has many things to commend it, but I doubt if many of its users view the main sports hall as a Place of Enlightenment. Kano also says that 'the dojo is not the place for idle talk or frivolous behaviour'. I quoted this to Keith recently, I forget why exactly — something to do with flatulence, possibly — and a defensive look flitted across his face. 'Well, we're not in Japan, are we?' he replied.

Many of the moves we use in judo, if you trace them back far enough, have probably got something to do with the flow of chi.

Some players doubtless practise their judo with this in mind. We used to have a Buddhist in our club, and there was a spiritual dimension to his judo. Once, when we were working on grips, I was paired with him. He was a slippery devil and I spent 99 per cent of the time getting a grip on a handful of air. In the end I asked, 'How do you *do* that?' He explained that it was to do with yin and yang, and that he was getting in touch with the feminine principle. Maybe that's where I was going wrong: I was too busy trying to get in touch with my macho side.

So what do I think Jesus would do? I think he'd approve. After all, wrestling is God's sport of choice. I'm basing this on the biblical account in Genesis of Jacob wrestling, and the fact that God did not engage Jacob in a round of golf, or in a keepy-uppy contest.

Jacob, if you remember, was the conniving weasel who tricked his older brother, Esau, out of his birthright and conned his blind father into giving him the crucial paternal blessing. Knowing that Esau was after his blood, Jacob fled. Over the course of many years he made his fortune, and eventually began to ponder his return and a possible reconciliation with his brother. The wrestling episode takes place when Jacob is nearly home. He has sent his wives, children, servants and livestock on ahead of him across the stream of Jabbok. His head is full of strategies to placate Esau when he meets him, as he surely will, the following day.

'And Jacob was left alone,' the text says. This was the valley of the shadow of death for poor old Jacob. He has already begged: 'Deliver me, I pray thee, from the hand of my brother, from the hand of Esau, for I fear him, lest he come and slay us all, the mothers with the children.' Now he is left alone with his terror in the pitch black of a Middle Eastern night. This, we might conclude, would be God's cue to appear and say something reassuring like, 'Fear not, my child! Behold, I will deliver you out of the hand of your brother Esau! Yea, he shall not harm a hair of your head, neither yours nor the mothers and children with you!'

Instead God attacks him — in the form of a stranger.[1]

I'm rather hoping we are not supposed to read this as a template for all spiritual

---

[1] This shadowy figure is popularly described as an angel, although the text simply says that 'a man wrestled with him'. Afterwards, however, Jacob states, 'I have seen God face to face.' In the Old Testament 'the Lord' and 'the angel of the Lord' are frequently synonymous.

experience. You're at your lowest ebb, God (or God's agent) stomps on you. It looks instead as if it's all to do with the kind of man Jacob was: a grasping cheat. It's more a case of 'OK. If that's the way you want it, that's the way it's going to be.'

The text is spare and elegant. 'And a man wrestled with him until the breaking of the day.' Hold it! says the novelist in me. Let's dramatise this a bit. Was Jacob asleep? Did he hear his assailant coming? What was going on in his mind? I bet he thought it was Esau! Was it completely dark, or was there moonlight? Could he see a vague shape, a glint of an eye? And the judo player in me says, Hold it! They wrestled *all night*?! I'm knackered after four minutes. All night and no score — they must have been pretty evenly matched. Didn't they stop for a breather and a drink? And look, the man sees he's not winning, so he puts Jacob's hip out of joint — that's got to be a prohibited act.

My friend Liz is a physiotherapist.[1] She is also a lay reader at the church we went to in

---

[1] She did judo with me for a while, and thoroughly enjoyed it until we got on to armlocks. She couldn't bear to do what flew in the face of all her professional training, so she gave up.

Walsall, and she was preaching on this very passage a while back. Her conclusion was that the Bible commentary writers were not anatomists, as they make very little of the innocent phrase which says the man/angel 'touched the hollow of his thigh; and Jacob's thigh was put out of joint'. Apparently, the hip joint is the largest, most stable joint in the body, held in place by the strongest tendons and biggest muscles. It takes a major trauma to dislocate it — a car smash, say. Some 'touch'. *Definitely* a prohibited act. *Hansoku make*, God: You're disqualified!

The other thing that strikes me, as a judo player, is that Jacob must have managed to get a good grip. The phrase 'Get a grip!' has a whole new dimension for me these days. It's not a metaphor — it's literal. If you don't get a grip, your opponent will slaughter you. When all else fails, hang on. Hang on for dear life. I reckon that's what Jacob was doing, even with his dislocated hip, because the stranger says, 'Let me go, for the day is breaking.' And Jacob replies, 'I will not let you go unless you bless me.' That's what the whole Jacob saga is all about: getting the blessing. He gets it, but he will limp forever after.

Getting a Grip

You can spot a judo player by their knuckles; especially the first set, nearest the nails. They will be knobbly and arthritic-looking, deformed. This comes from month after month of gripping the tough cotton jacket of your opponent. Sometimes my knuckles bleed if I've had a few weeks off training, but after a bit they toughen up again. The raw patches turn to scabs, the scabs to calluses. I look at my hands and think, they may not be pretty, but they are strong. I can cling on like a pit bull.

When you begin judo, you will be taught the conventional grip: right hand on opponent's left lapel, left hand on their sleeve. As you progress, you will learn alternatives. Sometimes your coach will devote part of a training session to the art of fighting for a grip. One person will attack while the other defends. Maybe you will be trying to get a sleeve grip, or maybe a high collar grip. There is also something called the 'pocket' grip, which is the front part of the jacket where surplus material bulges out from under the arms. In a mixed club this is the moment to sublimate all carnal thoughts — or better still, choose a partner of the same sex — since to the untrained eye this exercise looks for all the world like high-speed groping.

At different times I have favoured different grips. I often grab a handful of jacket round the back of my opponent's left shoulder, as it blocks off their left arm and hampers their attacks. They may then waste time trying to break my grip, time they would otherwise be using to throw me. Or they may become frustrated and lose their focus, perhaps leaving themselves vulnerable. Some players like to dominate from the start of a contest. They get a grip and throw off it. Others are patient and wily. They block and thwart you, working steadily for the grip they want.

Once someone has got their favourite grip, you are probably in trouble. This is why we also practise breaking an opponent's grip. (No biting, scratching or bending fingers back, of course.) There are several methods, all requiring such a sudden yanking action that the gripper may lose their fingernails if they stubbornly refuse to loose their hold.

Getting a grip and knowing when to let go — two valuable life skills courtesy of judo. They aren't taught explicitly, you have to make your own connections. I probably make too many of these, forever seeking out symbolic importance in stuff that barely merits a moment's consideration. 'You do tend to overanalyse things,' Debbie told me recently. 'Do I? Perhaps I do,' I said, plunging into another complex inward debate.

The truth is, you don't suddenly become a different person when you don a judo kit. Change happens gradually. By the time you are a green belt, you will be developing those judo knuckles. Your shoulders will be a bit more powerful. Your sense of balance will have improved. You will have toughened up. Hard landings are no longer a shock to the system. Driven A-type personalities may even be learning how to accommodate failure in their world view.

Green belt begins to feel as if you are getting somewhere. Below are yellow and orange, above are blue and brown. Then it's black. If it continues to go well, who knows — maybe you'll be a black belt in a few years. Unfortunately, progress tends to be more rapid in the earlier stages. This can give you the wrong impression. That's what happened to me. When I went to my very first grading, I bypassed orange altogether and came away with a green belt. This was because I won both my bouts, and the second was against an opponent who had already beaten someone else.

My first contest was brief. After a bit of ineffectual shoving around, we both ended up on the ground. My opponent made the novice's classic mistake of lifting her chin up while on all fours, so I slipped an arm across her throat from behind and put on what's called the 'naked strangle' (*hadakajime*).[1]

I was pretty confident I'd put the technique on properly and was surprised when she didn't submit. Funny, I said to myself, increasing the pressure. The ref was watching intently. Surely it's working! I thought in mounting agitation, looking up at him pleadingly, willing him to call *matte*. In the end, I couldn't stand it any more, and squeamishly let go. My opponent slumped apparently lifeless onto the mat. The next two minutes, after the medics had rushed on to revive her, were among the worst of my life. (This includes the time I dropped my baby on his head at the clinic in front of all the health visitors.)

While the flurry of medical activity was going on, I had to kneel on the mat and wait. This is normal etiquette, not a form of punishment. I managed not to cry. This was because I'd had a bit of practice biting back the tears during the previous week when I'd

---

[1] This isn't as exciting as it sounds, being 'naked' only in the sense that you don't use any part of the jacket or collar, simply your forearm. In other strangles the collar acts like a garotte.

tossed someone off the mat and she'd landed on her face. 'Don't *you* start crying!' said Keith in exasperation. 'Judo's a rough old sport. She knows that, or she wouldn't be here.'

Eventually, I was bowed off the mat by the ref. When my opponent was finally up and walking around again, I went across to apologise. 'Are you OK?' I asked. 'Yes, I've lost my voice, though,' she whispered. Good. That made me feel better. I hadn't killed her, I'd only pulverised her larynx.

I think now would be a good time to break off and have a little section called:

How to Submit

This is *very important*. In judo you signal submission (i.e. giving in) by tapping your opponent, or the mat, a couple of times. You can tap any part of their anatomy that is handy. If both your arms are pinned, slap the mat with your feet. Alternatively, you can say, '*Matte!*' Should all your limbs be pinioned and your mouth stuffed full of your opponent's *judogi*, pray.

If you are sensible, you submit well before your arm gets broken or you pass out. I'm very quick to submit if someone has a good

168

armlock on. I have never been particularly flexible and so am quite susceptible to these techniques. Some players are double-jointed. This is tiresome. You get to know who they are, and you don't waste your time trying to armlock them, you just throttle them instead. If you are strong you will be able to resist an armlock to a certain extent, but once you know you're at the point of no return, you may as well tap — unless you are a samurai warrior and submission would oblige you to commit *seppuku*. Better a broken arm than your guts sprawling out all over the place, I suppose.[1]

Strangles are a slightly different matter. There are two basic types: chokes (for example, *hadaka-jime*), which shut off the windpipe and are effective almost immediately; and true strangles, which put pressure on the carotid arteries, thus cutting off the supply of oxygen to the brain. Oh, how I love judo! Just as some players are double-jointed, so you will also discover that others (i.e. most blokes) have powerful necks. You'd have as much joy trying to strangle a telegraph pole,

---

[1] The Japanese champion Kashiwazaki once famously allowed his arm to be broken rather than face the dishonour of tapping out.

so don't bother, just drive your knee into his *kogans*.[1]

A good choke should get a quick submission, but strangles come on more gradually — say between five and ten seconds. The temptation here is to try and ride the strangle instead of submitting, and in the meantime, attempt some technique of your own. This is a trap that men are prone to fall into when being strangled by women. I imagine the thought process goes something like this: 'Pff! It's only a girl, I'll just flex my neck muscles. OK, quick turnover into *kesa* and . . . zonk . . . Huh? What happened?'

★ ★ ★

Back to my first grading. My second contest was against a clubmate who'd been watching my earlier fight. The bout was brief. After a bit of ineffectual shoving around, we both ended up on the ground. She made the novice's classic mistake of lifting her chin up while on all fours, so I slipped an arm across her throat from behind and —

She submitted instantly.

Afterwards, when all the novices had

---

[1] I do beg your pardon. That was a typo for 'try something else instead'.

bowed off the mat, we got changed then waited around while the referees conferred and entered their decisions in the back of our licences. This was the start of the official record of our progress. At every grading we would hand our little black books in with our fee, and they would be returned to us when the ordeal was over, containing the good news or the bad.

I was anticipating good news, and was surprised when the examiner handed me my licence with the stern words, 'You need to do some more theory.' I took this to imply, 'So that you won't endanger anyone else's life ever again, you lunatic.' In fact, all he meant was that although I'd been awarded a bottom green belt, I had only done the theory up as far as top orange. I would not actually be entitled to wear my new green belt until I'd demonstrated the next set of techniques and duly had my licence signed by my coach.

I remember leaving the sports stadium in the summer sunshine and ringing my husband from the car park with the good news. I then sat for a while grinning and thinking, Wow! Incredible! I'm a green belt! That wasn't so bad after all.

This was back when judo was still fun. It will be fun again, I'm sure. It will, it will! — once this black-belt nonsense is over.

***

Judo can be a lot more fun if you are just spectating. Suddenly it's a breeze. You can see exactly when to change direction, when to feint. All the right throws and counters are blindingly obvious. And there's no risk of getting hurt. Your enjoyment will be enhanced by an understanding of how the scoring system works. Back in the mists of time there was only one score in judo: *ippon*. *Ippon* means 'one', or 'full score'. This is the true Samurai Way — either/or, sudden death. These days this has been tempered by the introduction of other, lesser scores. For convenience, an *ippon* is now reckoned to be a 10-point score and is awarded either for an out-and-out killer throw (where the victim — sorry, *uke* — lands flat on his or her back), or for a submission, or for a pin-down that lasts the full twenty-five seconds. Next comes *waza-ari*, which is a 7-point score. This might be given for a good, but not quite killer, throw. Perhaps the opponent manages to land on their side, rather than on their back. My BJA syllabus informs me that 'a 7-point score added to another 7-point score' — signalled by the ref shouting '*Waza-ari-awasete-ippon*' — will result in *ippon*. In gradings, these are the only scores awarded: 10, 7 or 7+7=10. (Don't worry about the maths; it's

172

probably Zen, or something.)[1]

At other contests smaller scores may also be awarded. *Yuko*, according to my syllabus, is given for a throw not quite as good as a *waza-ari*, or for a pindown lasting between twenty and twenty-five seconds. This is worth 5 points. *Koka* is a 3-point score awarded when 'the person thrown has landed on his thigh(s) or buttocks with speed or force'. Each of these scores is signalled by a different semaphore from the ref.

Alongside the scores are the penalties. The dastardly thing about penalties is that they are cumulative. If you get too many, you will be disqualified. Small scores, however, are not cumulative. The mathematics of judo dictates that *yuko+yuko* does not equal *ippon*. Neither does *koka+koka+koka+koka* and so on, la la la, forever. This doesn't seem fair to me, but I dare say that's because I have a woman's pulse.

Armed with this knowledge of how the scoring system works, we will find, to our dismay, that when we watch a judo contest, we still have no clear idea what is going on,

---

[1] Keith and Debbie maintain that there is also a score of '*wappon*', which is awarded when the ref changes his or her mind halfway between *waza-ari* and *ippon*.

who has scored, and why. *Ippon* is usually the most unambiguous, although you will sometimes see people standing round the mat sucking their teeth and shaking their heads. No way! That was only a *waza-ari*. Occasionally a ref will be overruled by a senior examiner. This happened during one of my bouts at the last grading. My opponent was awarded a *waza-ari* when I landed on my side, but this was immediately retracted on the grounds that she hadn't done a proper technique at all, I had merely fallen over her leg.

It's even trickier when both players land on the mat simultaneously. The ref and the corner judges will have to confer and decide who landed first, and whose technique it was. If both players were attempting a technique — say an attack and a counter — who contributed more? Was the player who landed on his/her back actually doing a sacrifice throw? It can get a bit subjective. I'm afraid the samurai would have had no patience with this kind of faffing around. Cut them all down!

Diary

8 July 2005

Grading tomorrow, and I have just done one of those things which I ought not to have done — picked up an injury during training. I was doing some gentle practice with my son and threw him, and he landed on my foot. At first I thought it was just one of those Ow-ow-ow! hopping around type of things, but it's now several hours later, and it's pretty painful. I'm assuming it won't prevent me from going tomorrow, but it's certainly not going to help. I rubbed arnica all over the bruise, but I doubt that's enough. Bloody hell. Pete offered me his ankle support. I'm not sure. It would advertise to less scrupulous players that you are carrying an injury. I suppose there's nothing to do except see how it is in the morning.

The kit is ironed and the bag ready to pack. I went for a gentle jog round the block first thing this morning (keeping an eye out for dogs as my last wound has barely healed), more as a mood lifter than anything else. I've managed to keep my spirits up reasonably well this time, so I'll be frustrated not to have a go. Part of me would be glad of the let-out, but long term it's no answer. I've been reading the second instalment of Lance Armstrong's biography, *Every Second Counts*. 'Pain is temporary, quitting lasts forever,' he says. Maybe I should have that on a T-shirt. It's what got me through my doctorate.

19 July 2005
Nul points. The gap between this entry and the last was to give me time to sulk.

I had four fights and lost them all. This is quite common. Not many players get all the way to 1st dan without losing a single bout. But it hadn't happened to me before. In a way I'm glad. If I'd been so comprehensively beaten at my first black belt attempt, I don't know how I'd have had the courage to have another go. I met one woman there who'd got nothing at her first three.

When I woke on Sunday I discovered that I could walk on my injured ankle without difficulty. Damn! This removed the only honourable reason for not going.

I tried to make myself write up what had happened while it was still raw, but although a lot of people use writing as a means of exorcising the bad stuff, I never do. Instead I process it in my head by sitting and thinking and praying and reading, or maybe by talking it over with a friend or my spiritual director. Writing for me is an escape from anguish, not a form of catharsis. I don't want my sacred space polluted by life's rubbish. Years later, of course, some of it resurfaces as fiction, but only after undergoing a sea change into something (I hope) rich and strange.

But after that interesting build-up, I have to confess that the grading wasn't *that* bad, really. I just didn't have my fighting head on. There were six of us on the 'ladies' 1st kyu mat. After we'd bowed on, I slunk over to the judges' table and mentioned that I was a veteran. The examiner showed me the list of ages. I was the only vet. The next oldest was twenty-six. All he could do, he told me, was make sure my first bout was against the lightest opponent. I'd love to claim that it was my age that let me down, but, sadly, stamina isn't really an issue if you are beaten as swiftly as I was.

My best chance was definitely in the first fight. I was close to throwing her a couple of times, and she was a bit lucky to get an *ippon* for the throw that ended the match. In my opinion. Blood from the dog bite began seeping through my trousers. My ankle ached. On the next mat to ours the 1st kyu men were battling it out, dozens of them, locking horns like monarchs of the glen. Lloyd got his last 10 points for his 1st dan. I wish Neil could have seen it.

My next bout lasted less than a minute. I managed to ride one throw, but was then taken out by a well-executed *o-goshi*. After that I lost heart. I was cannon fodder. Here, everybody — have 10 points on me! In my head I could hear Keith telling me I needed to go up a gear. But there wasn't one left in the box. All I had was neutral. I went numbly through the motions till it was all over and we bowed off the mat.

If I were a proper sportsperson, I'd be analysing this in great detail. Where did I go wrong? Where can I improve? I'm wondering how I can convey just how extreme my reluctance is to engage with this. If I search my soul I discover a voice saying, Sod it, I just lost, OK? The most helpful response now is to forget all about it. The worst bit is that this means more gradings.

Swiftly, for the record, I lost the third match to what my opponent described afterwards as two 'crappy drop-knees' which both got *waza-ari*. In the final bout — against a young woman who had travelled down from Newcastle and got her 1st dan all in one go on the day — I was pinned down by my old favourite, *kesa-gatame*. For which, according to Keith, I want slapping, because we'd spent ages working on escapes.

I was not on fire. But what can you do about that? Apart from contacting the BJA with the request that they please schedule the next grading to coincide with a more hormonally favourable part of the month. Paula Radcliffe uses the pill to shift her period so that she's on peak form at major sporting events. This relies on forward planning and having a better grasp of your cycle than simply noticing that your boobs hurt and you are shouting at everybody through mouthfuls of trashy carbohydrate.

Would praying help? 'O thou who camest from above, / The pure celestial fire to impart. / Kindle a flame of sacred love / On the mean altar of my heart.' Yet again, the Christian model is unsuited to martial arts. Wesley's pure celestial fire of sacred love is not the same as having fire in your belly. I have trouble thinking how such a petition might go: 'Dear Lord, help me slaughter my opponents today. Let them lose. Prosper the work of my hands. If it be Thy will, of course.'

So, I'm too nice. But I don't want to stop being me and become nasty and unkind in order to get my black belt. I talked about this a bit with Keith and he says this is partly his and Debbie's fault. They don't train us up to be mean. But if they did, I probably wouldn't have stuck with judo.

This, not stamina, is the real disadvantage to being a veteran. Judo is not just about fighting. It has gathered too many accretions. *Life* has gathered too many accretions. Nothing's ever just about one thing any more. It's about all the places you have been and all that's happened to you as well. I'm like a ship encrusted with barnacles. *That's* what it's like. It's not emotional baggage, bags and cases you can dump if you're disciplined enough. It's emotional bloody barnacles. They have an entire ecosystem going. It would take years to scrape them off.

All I can think is that if I keep pegging away, I will improve, or get lucky enough times, or encounter enough other crap players. That's how I'm feeling at the moment — like a crap player. I took the trouble to ask the judge afterwards to explain the points system. At the moment I still need 100 points, not the 70 I'd thought. A year after getting my 1st kyu (i.e. next February) it comes down to 75 points. Six months after that it comes down to 50 points. So if I've got 40 more points by next August, I will have got enough for my dan grade. That sounds doable, doesn't it? Yeah, I can do that. Pain is temporary. Quitting lasts forever.

★ ★ ★

I walked back from the judo centre after it was all over. It's a couple of miles to St Paul's, and I didn't feel too bad, really. It was a hot day. The air was full of lime blossom. Short of getting injured, that was as bad as it gets, and I'd survived. I'd given it a go. I hadn't cried. I'd been brave and gracious in defeat.

As I walked the last stretch down Leicester Street I caught myself thinking, This has made me *more* determined, not less. In which case, the experience was not wasted. I like to think nothing ever is. Nothing wasted, nothing lost. Just the occasional thing you'd avoid if you were given the choice.

5

Blue Belt

Jesus, good above all other,
Gentle child of gentle mother,
In a stable born our brother,
Give us grace to persevere.

Hymn 43, 'Jesus, Good Above All Other'
in *With Cheerful Voice: Hymns for Children*

When the Going Gets Tough

Oh, I'm fed up with all this hard work, all this
going out running and not eating cake and
facing my fears and being humiliated and
hurt and losing and picking myself up and
losing again. I'm off to JJB Sports to buy
myself a black belt BECAUSE I'M WORTH
IT. Go on — treat yourself. You deserve it,
Catherine! You can be anything you want.
Have a makeover and become a dan grade.
Project that image of yourself, *believe* in
yourself.

Sport is quaintly old-fashioned nowadays. Despite all the hype and glamour, it's one of those areas of modern life where hard work and talent are still rewarded. With the possible exceptions of Eddie the Eagle and the Jamaican bobsleigh team, you can't be famous in sport just for being famous. You have to be good as well. While there are lucky breaks, there are no short cuts. On the sports field and in the dojo, this L'Oréal bollocks doesn't wash. I may think I *deserve* an Olympic gold medal, or a place in the Newcastle squad, but that's not going to get me one. Maybe sport in schools is more important now, in our wannabe culture, than it ever has been before. Taking part in sport provides a dose of realism. No pain, no gain. There simply is no sporting equivalent of winning the lottery, no overnight success without putting in the work.

The importance of persevering is something I came to late in my life. As a child I was never inclined to waste time practising something I wasn't instantly brilliant at. I've now reached the stage in my judo where it is no longer simply great fun and plain sailing. 'Give us grace to persevere,' as the old hymn says. Deep down I am still tempted by the grace of instant brilliance instead, but that is not on offer.

I used to think of blue belt as the halfway point to black. I now realise that this is an optical illusion. You probably have to win about as many fights to get your 1st dan as you did to get to top brown in the first place. (Unless you are OLD, ha ha, when the bar is compassionately dropped.)[1] But the minute you get your brown belt, you can't help thinking you are practically there. A couple more gradings, you tell yourself while you are still surfing that endorphin wave, and I'll do it. When people ask what belt you are, you start saying, 'Brown. Which is the one before black.' And they reply, 'Well, I won't argue with *you* then.'

I still have a soft spot for blue belt, however. Getting one was a childhood ambition of mine. Blue was my favourite colour, so blue belt was second only to black in my mind. Brown belt was *theoretically* better, but it was only a necessary evil you passed through on the way to black. Blue was

---

[1] I spoke too soon. The BJA has changed the rules again. There are no longer any concessions for veterans (over thirty for women, thirty-five for men — a piece of sexism I've decided to overlook). For veterans already fighting for their dan grade there is an amnesty till the beginning of 2008.

the point at which you might begin to say to yourself, Hey, I'm pretty good at this. People had better start taking notice. My mate Cindy from primary school got as far as blue belt. She was in the same club at Tunnel Cement, but her family moved to Surrey when we were both about thirteen, and she joined a club there and started doing very well indeed. She even had a trial for the national squad, but training clashed with after-school remedial physics at her convent, and her dad put his foot down. I wonder what she thinks about this now. Which is the more useful life skill — O-level Physics, or Olympic-level judo? And did she ever get the O level after all that?

The BJA syllabus seems to go up a gear at blue-belt level. Suddenly you are expected to demonstrate sacrifice throws. To the novice these techniques look as if they've escaped from a scary martial-arts movie. Wow! I'll never be able to do that, I used to think. *Kata-guruma* (shoulder wheel), another blue-belt technique, is a bit like a fireman's lift. Or like a fireman's lift might end up, if you were foolish enough to annoy the fireman. I thought I'd never be able to do that throw, either. And funnily enough, I never did. Except once, flukily, when called upon to demonstrate it for my licence. On my first attempt I buckled under my opponent's weight. This was the only occasion when I've known Keith guffaw tactlessly at a crap technique. (He normally says something affirming like, 'That was excellent! Now try it again completely differently in every possible respect from what you just did.')

I wasn't a blue belt for very long. My progress through the lower grades was rapid. But I got stuck on brown belt for a very long time — still am at the time of writing this chapter, in fact — for a variety of reasons, some more feeble than others. One of the factors was my time in New Zealand.

Where the Wild Things Are — The New Zealand Months

I grew up in a churchgoing family. Technically, it was a chapelgoing family, since we were Baptists. I remained a Baptist until I finally went over to Canterbury in my mid-twenties. At one stage, when I was about ten, we had a minister called Dr Hodge. After many years working in New Zealand, he and his wife retired to Berkhamsted, which wasn't far from our chapel in Tring. (After a few years they realised they were mad, and re-retired to New Zealand, and who can blame them?) One harvest supper they treated us to a slide show of their time in the Land of the Long White Cloud, and from then on New Zealand, with its volcanic mud pools, glow-worm caves and Maori culture, became a magical place in my imagination.

The Hodges had a glass-fronted cabinet in their sitting room full of souvenirs from their travels. When we visited them, we were allowed to look at the treasures. I remember one rainy afternoon holding a paua shell, a special kind of vivid-coloured abalone found only in New Zealand waters. I ached to walk on the beach and find one of my own. I called my pet rabbit Hinemoa, after the Maori princess. I wrote a project on New Zealand. I even put a glow-worm cave in my novel *Wild Cat's Gang*.

This is probably why, when my husband was entitled to extended study leave in 2002 and floated the possibility of spending it in New Zealand, I astonished him by saying, 'Great! I've always wanted to go there.' My normal stance on travel is a resistance to anywhere I haven't already been, and to offer twenty reasons why any new destination is impossible, or frankly dangerous. The tug of New Zealand even overcame the difficulties involved in taking our children out of school for three months.[1]

New Zealand strikes the British visitor as strange, yet simultaneously familiar. This familiarity is more than a sense of déjà vu created by the well-known three-part travel advert, *The Lord of the Rings*. People often say New Zealand is like England was in the fifties, which is unfair, as Kiwi life and culture has moved on a great deal (though the quieter bits of the South Island have only just reached the seventies). The place does feel undeniably and nostalgically like home. Just as you are reminiscing, though, it will jolt you by its utter strangeness.

As you, the British visitor, pootle along (without the headache of remembering to drive on the right), the landscape will remind you of the west coast of Scotland. Except there's no heather. Then you notice something that resembles heather, only it's ten feet tall. Or maybe there is English-looking farmland with neat hedges and herds of cows. English-looking, if you fail to spot that the

---

[1] Here's an interesting thing: if you take your kids out of school a week early so you can get cheap flights to Tuscany, this is bad. If, instead, you take them out of school for three whole months, it becomes an excellent educational opportunity.

edges of the fields are smoking quietly and seeping sulphurous fumes. In the garden there are blackbirds singing, just like back home. Then suddenly you hear a wild haunting snatch of birdsong like a flute concerto played in Eden. But at least the towns are reassuringly called Wellington, Nelson, New Plymouth, Hamilton. Well, apart from when they are called something like Whakarewarewa.[1]

Most of our time was spent in the capital, Wellington, which is at the south of the North Island. We'd arranged a house swap over the Internet with a recently retired couple, Graham and Nancy. Our borrowed house looked down over Wellington Harbour, so I could sit and read Janet Frame and watch the constantly changing light on the water and the mountain ranges across the bay, the little yachts leaning on the wind, inter-island ferries coming and going, luxury liners docking, and the occasional pod of killer whales — a pretty good exchange for a view across Mellish Road, Walsall, I thought.

Graham and Nancy weren't complaining, mind you. This is because they are Kiwis and their default mode is 'Wow! Brilliant!' We

---

[1] Short for Te Whakarewarewatanga-o-te-ope-Taua-a-Wahiao, but generally known as Whaka.

189

gradually got used to this as we toured the North and South Islands. When you stop to buy petrol, the garage owner typically bounces up, fills your tank, asks where you've come from, then says something like, 'Hey, fantastic! Isn't it a great place? Where are you heading? Oh, wow! Fantastic! You'll love it!' Nancy and Graham had the opposite experience. Nobody in Walsall could work out why on earth they were visiting. When pressed, people admitted that they quite liked living here themselves, it was just that they couldn't see why anyone else would bother to come.

New Zealand is as an interesting social experiment in what happens to a bunch of Scots if you transplant them to the opposite side of the globe and shine a bit of sun on them. They lay aside their customary dour outlook. They become cheery and outgoing. They forget Culloden and stop hating the English. They hate the Aussies instead. New Zealand friendliness does take a bit of getting used to, mind you. When you enter a shop the assistants greet you so effusively — 'HI!!! How are YOU today?' — you instinctively check behind you to see who they are talking to.

It was this kind of open-hearted welcome that awaited me in the Wellington Judo and Jujitsu Academy. Unfortunately, it meant that it was a while before it fully dawned on me what I had blundered into. Perhaps I should have been alerted early on when I went to buy a *judogi* at Wellington's martial-arts shop. The club was recommended by the guy who'd served me. He admitted that there was another club nearby. 'For people who like their judo easy,' he added a little contemptuously. I remember thinking, That sounds like me. Always listen to your inner voices. When I rang the contact number I'd been given, the man who answered sounded a bit thoughtful. 'What grade are you?' he asked. 'Brown belt? Oh, well, you should be OK.'

And I was OK. Just. Here's an extract from the journal I kept:

Went to my first judo session last night at the Wellington Judo Academy. They are mad. Or rather, they are Kiwis, and train like maniacs. Even if I hadn't had 6 weeks off to eat like a hog, I'd have struggled to keep up. Still, I hope to train 3 times a week and go home a killing machine — or in a box. They were all very friendly and welcoming and I hope to be less feeble as time goes on.

The next session seems to have gone a bit better:

It wasn't quite so crippling last night, perhaps because the senior coach wasn't there and one of the brown belts took the session. Still felt pretty battered, but not about to vomit or pass out coughing up blood.

The dojo was on the third floor of a building on College Street, near Courtney Place and the big cinema where *The Lord of the Rings* was premiered. We arrived in January of 2003, just after part two had been released, and a vast model of Gollum still loomed from the roof, reaching out for a huge replica of the One Ring. *LOTR* fever was running high, and after a while it began to worry me they didn't know Tolkien was English, actually.

It was summer, and often stiflingly hot up there in the dojo. Occasionally I even hankered after a British January. The floor was permanently matted, so at least we were spared *tatami-waza*, that knackering form of training better known as 'putting the mats away'. It wasn't a purpose-built dojo, however. There was a pillar in the middle of the room. It may have been amply padded, but it was still disconcerting to find yourself hurtling towards it head first.

The premises were shared with a boxing

club and there was a small ring at the far end. Sometimes, as I climbed the final flight of stairs, I could hear the chains on the punchbags jingling. It sounded exactly like a tambourine troop going full throttle. I was disappointed it wasn't, really, because the juxtaposition of martial arts and the Sally Army girls with their ribbons and bonnets might have been interesting. The punchbags would continue to move and creak softly until they finally fell silent long after anyone had finished using them. I see from my journal that the sound made me think of lynched corpses swinging from trees in the wind. Which probably tells you something about my frame of mind.

In a way, my time at the club was a paradigm of my whole New Zealand experience: superficial familiarity masking profound foreignness. The sessions were usually run by Kevin, who I secretly referred to as Kommandant Kevin, until I got to know him a bit better and started thinking of him as Kaiser instead. Yep, he worked us hard. 'Who said anything about stopping?' he would yell. 'This isn't a holiday camp!' Most of the players were blokes, and most of them were brown belts. In my three months there only two other women came along. One was an exquisite petite student, who, despite being from Japan, was a novice. The other was an exquisite petite blonde, also a novice, who used to wear a tiny red vest and red tartan bra under her jacket. In comparison, I, at a sweating 70kg and wearing my clapped-out grey T-shirt, was one of the blokes. *Be nice, Cethy!* they would admonish me, whenever I was fighting Makoto or Hannah. A brown belt called Cameron took me under his wing, kindly driving me home when he could, and discussing New Zealand literature with me, or dishing the dirt on New Zealand judo's more colourful characters.

If you were late you had to do press-ups, a certain number (which trauma appears to have blanked from my memory — 10? 20? 200?) for each five minutes of training you'd missed.[1] Sometimes we were paired off and had to do as many throws, alternately, as we could manage in two minutes (i.e. throw, be thrown, get up, throw, be thrown, get up, throw, be thrown, lie there, get hauled up by

---

[1] Once I got on the wrong bus and it stopped a good mile and a half short of the dojo. I looked so terrified at the prospect of being late that the driver took pity on me, put the 'Out of Service' sign on and drove me there anyway. I'm telling you — Kiwi bus drivers are the nicest in the world.

angry partner, throw, be thrown, lie there, sob brokenly, etc.). Kevin would then go round the room making us call out how many throws we'd done. The pair who'd managed the least had to do more press-ups as a punishment. All counting out loud was done in Japanese, which I had never learned. I went in dread of being asked to count and repeatedly got my older son to coach me. I never mastered beyond four. (You can't memorise new stuff after childbirth. It's a medical fact.) The only time we were asked to number off down the line in Japanese I was miraculously and blessedly standing fourth in the row. *Ichi, ni, san, SHI!* Thank you, Jesus!

We'd begin the session by warming up, jogging round the mat for about as long as I'd normally spend on my morning run. Then there would be stretches, press-ups, squat thrusts, rolling breakfalls, commando crawling, cartwheels, or simply dragging yourself across the mat using your arms alone. Everyone had to stand waiting for me, as I was always last. Anyone paired with me was also last, or did the least number of throws and ended up doing press-ups (while I lay on the mat incapacitated and trembling after one press-up and feeling like Judas).

What came next was a blur of drills, *uchi komi* (repeat practice throwing), *randori* and

195

me being splatted onto my back so many times I couldn't see straight. On the first night I seriously thought I was going to throw up on the mat. This is extremely bad etiquette. You're supposed to vomit inside your own jacket. Or failing that, inside the jacket of the highest grade player on the mat. After a few sessions one of the other coaches, a revered sensei in his seventies called Patrick,[1] took me to one side and said kindly, 'Take a rest whenever you need to. Nobody expects you to keep up with these brutes.' Nobody except me, I thought.

Now there are judo clubs and judo clubs wherever you go. If you are a visiting Kiwi (or just a mad bastard), I dare say you could find yourself plenty of dojos in the UK where they work you this hard. But as Keith often says, 'We like to take it steady.' It's not *just* because I was a wimpy Pom in New Zealand that I found it tough. Though that accounts for a good deal of it, I fear. 'This is an entire nation on a self-imposed commando training

---

[1] Age had not withered his technique, nor custom staled its infinite variety. His stamina was the only thing that occasionally let him down, and the others ruthlessly exploited this. 'Make the old man run!' they would shout when someone was fighting him.

course,' warns Pete McCarthy in his book, *McCarthy's Bar*. 'New Zealanders will never walk up or down something if there's a chance it will hurt more to run instead.'

Most Brits who visit New Zealand love the place. Quite a few up sticks and emigrate there. We discovered this accidentally by enthusing to local people, 'This is a great country you've got here!' and having them reply, 'Um, yes. Actually, I'm from Kent.' The only real reservation expats seem to have is about being constantly pestered with invitations to go free-fall black-water shark fishing every weekend, when all they really want to do is stay in and watch the telly.

The New Zealand national motto seems to be 'Give it a go!' I told this to our curate Simon when we got back home, and he said, 'Yes, and ours is, 'I'd be crap at that.' ' This may be partly why I tried so hard to keep up with the brutes during all those training sessions: to uphold (female) British honour. There was one awful occasion when I blurted out, 'I can't do that!' before I'd even attempted something. Hannah, who I was paired with for the exercise, looked shocked. I can't remember what it was now — dragging myself the length of the mat with my lips before doing forty one-arm press-ups with my partner on my back? Actually, shocked isn't quite the word. She looked appalled and compassionate and embarrassed all at once, as though I'd just confided that I'd wet myself. 'Well, we can give it go, eh,' she said, and I was shamed into making the attempt.

Giving Him Something to Think About — The Art of the Borderline Technique

We now move on to a tricky section. Tricky for me to write, just in case any of the nice chaps from the Wellington Judo and Jujitsu Academy decide to come across to the UK and look me up. And tricky because I never really let myself think about it during my time at the club. Basically, the issue is this: they taught and used dirty tactics. There. I've come out with it. Even now, at a safe distance both geographically and chronologically, I find it hard to admit, because they were great guys and I liked them a lot. Dirty tactics? Big deal! you might be thinking. But for me it really *is* a big deal. Debbie and Keith make us aware of underhand techniques, just in case we come up against them in a contest, but they don't promote them (unless someone does it to us first, in which case, they asked for it). Fight hard, but fight fair.[1]

This is why I spent so much of my time in Wellington squeaking, 'Isn't that illegal?' My clubmates would give me a blank psychotic stare, then reply, 'Well, yeah, *technically*, you nit-picking Pommie wimp.' (The last bit was implied.) It turned out that things were illegal 'only if the ref sees'. These new techniques were generally introduced under the heading of giving your opponent 'something to think about'. This wasn't as cerebral and abstract as it sounds. 'Make sure you work your knuckles into his thigh muscle/kneel on his kidneys, give him something to think about.'

One of the club experts was Brian. His reputation as the Prince of Darkness preceded him. I'd been to the club several times before I met him, and I was alerted to his arrival one night by my literary friend Cameron: 'By the pricking of my thumbs, something wicked this way comes.' For some reason I never fathomed — and which may not be sinister at all — Brian was still a brown belt, though he was clearly operating at dan-grade level. Once when I was fighting him at groundwork, he was briefly on his feet. This should mean the bout ends and we

---

[1] Come to think of it, God was a worryingly dirty fighter in the Jacob narrative (see above).

stand up, so I complained that he was cheating. He gave me a beatific smile and said, 'You'll notice I cheat a lot.' On another occasion we were practising a move that looked to me very much like throwing someone when you'd got an armlock on them, which is strictly verboten. This wasn't what it was at all, apparently, though I could never quite master the distinction. '*Surely* that's illegal!' I bleated. But no, it was what was known in the club as 'a borderline technique'.[1]

This stuff goes on in the UK too, of course. I'm not in any way trying to perpetuate a racial stereotype. The interesting thing, reading my journal now, is the extent to which I couldn't admit to myself what was going on. I'm very bad at reading social situations at the best of times. This may sound like an odd confession from a novelist: you'd imagine we'd all be shrewd observers

---

[1] To be fair, there are techniques too borderline even for them. I had a letter from Cameron a while ago telling me they'd had a visit from a 5th dan called Mike Bond. 'He showed me a few tricks which I will bear in mind next time somebody comes at me with a broken bottle, but will be sure to forget when I am in a tournament.' (If Mike would like to get in touch, I can tell him what else Cameron said.)

of human interaction. (This isn't the case. When we say we are sensitive, we mean you aren't allowed to criticise us in case we burst into tears.) I seem to have been born without that emotional barometer that enables most people to register 'an atmosphere'. If a couple tell me they are OK, I believe them, and will therefore fail to spot that they are acrimoniously divorcing one another before my very eyes. Likewise, if the bunch I meet at the dojo strike me as great guys (albeit a little manic about training), I will persist in thinking the best of them.

The truth dawned very gradually over those weeks of boot-camp-style training in the dark arts. I remember overhearing someone remark laughingly (in connection with the harsh lighting and number of cauliflower ears in the dojo), 'No wonder they think we're all animals!' Somehow, by the time I left, I had ended up with the distinct impression that at one stage the club had been ejected in disgrace from the Judo Association. I checked this with Cameron, and it turns out not to have been the case, after all. From the point of view of the present narrative, this is a real shame; but I am writing a work of non-fiction, so I'm not really supposed to make stuff up. I'm probably hampered by my academic background and by being married to a clergyman.

(And the thought of Brian coming over and breaking my arm in three places.) When asked, Cameron — having unfortunately got wind of the fact that I was writing a book about them[1] — issued a measured, not to say bland, statement to the effect that the club 'has not always enjoyed a harmonious relationship with the administration of Judo New Zealand'. He went on to dismiss it all as 'a storm in a very small teacup on a very small draining board on a very small kitchen bench on a very small archipelago in the South Pacific'. From which I conclude that a lot of really juicy stuff has been swept under the *tatami*.

If I'd known the dojo's reputation in advance, I might have stayed at home reading Janet Frame. I'm not just saying that. There are clubs here in the West Midlands I'm too scared to go to. Happily, this isn't a book about confronting my demons. It's about managing to carry on, somehow, in spite of being a bit of a coward — taking a long, circuitous route *around* my demons, if you like. But if I ever found myself back in Wellington, would I grab my *judogi* and head back to College Street? Yes, of course I would. Though I'd make very sure I wasn't late.

---

[1] This may have been my fault for saying, 'I'm writing a book about you lot.'

Because despite all that I've just said, I had a good time there.

Just as a treat, on my last night, they gave me a line-up. This means you get to fight everyone in the club in turn without a breather, starting with the lowest grade and working up to the highest. I knew Kevin would insist. It was what they did for fun when it was someone's birthday, instead of buying them a card. If I'm honest, I was feeling sick with dread. I even contemplated not turning up, but that would mean leaving without saying goodbye, and that would look rude and ungrateful, which would have been marginally worse. When the final session came, Kevin was stranded in Auckland by high winds after a trip north. See? God is good. Jason, who was taking the session instead, mercifully allowed me a groundwork line-up. (God is not a pushover, though.) I didn't win a single fight. But hey — I gave it a go.

I did learn a lot during my stay in New Zealand. My breakfalls improved no end. This is the happy by-product of being tossed repeatedly on your head. Not that you are supposed to land on your head: tuck and roll, tuck and roll. Sometimes if someone throws you incompetently, you will inevitably land badly. You may then console yourself with the knowledge that this makes it *their* fault, not yours. I remember one neck-crunching landing of this kind in Wellington. 'Oh, *Adrian!*' Cameron tutted, in the tones of mild exasperation I normally reserve for people who spill sugar on the kitchen work surface. Still, it gave me something to think about. Or might have done, but for the concussion.

My groundwork also improved. I learned not to curl up in a defensive position on all fours, hanging on to my collar and waiting for the ref to call *matte*, which is accepted practice in many clubs. In Wellington, a defensive posture was an invitation to a wide range of thought-provoking techniques, perhaps most elegantly summarised by Brian: 'If you do that, I will fucking kill you. I mean it.' It was essentially a *ne-waza* club. Groundwork was their thing. More specifically, 'tap outs' were their thing: forced submissions. Why win by throwing someone, when it's much more fun to win by forcing them to submit in excruciating agony? I learned how to fight strongly from the guard position (on my back with my opponent between my legs — don't be childish, we've discussed this already), in particular, how to use my legs to get a straight armlock on someone who is trying to strangle me. We practised this repeatedly as a drill. It's reassuring to know I still have a muscle memory. I'd assumed it had been ravaged long since by some form of Alzheimer's.

Keith thinks I came back from New Zealand as a much more defensive fighter. I expect he's right. After three months as the club *uke* I grew cautious. I needed to concentrate all my energies on not being thrown, and this became a habit. Blocking your opponent's attacks is a good skill to master, but on its own, it's not enough. You have to attack as well. This is not just because, as any fule kno, attack is the best form of defence. There are also rules governing 'passivity'. If you allow twenty seconds to go by in a contest without making a genuine attack, you will be penalised for non-combativity. The problem with attacking is that you lay yourself open to a counter-attack. The problem with *not* attacking (apart from picking up a penalty) is that you will probably get thrown.

One way or another you are vulnerable, so you may as well go for it. Giving it a go and taking a risk is integral to the Kiwi outlook.[1] I

_____

[1] A Kiwi friend suggested to me that their outlook was based on the brute fact of geography. 'If we don't give it a go ourselves, nobody's going to come and help us. We're so far from anywhere else.'

hope that some of it rubbed off on me. Gain without pain is not a basic human right, along with glossy hair. I'm worth more than that. You have to take risks in order to achieve anything. Nothing ventured, nothing gained. Mind you, now and then it will feel as though all you have gained for your venturing is pain and humiliation, but at least you tried.

In this respect, as in so many others, judo imitates life. There is whole suite of high-risk strategies you can employ on the mat. They are known as 'sacrifice throws'.

Sacrifice Throws

The best-known *sutemi-waza*, or sacrifice throw, is probably *tomoe-nage*, the stomach throw. If you are looking down complacently at your own ample beer belly, sorry to disappoint you: it's about your opponent's stomach. This is judo, not gut-barging. *Tomoe-nage* is one of the techniques you will need to demonstrate for your blue belt. It involves sacrificing your own balance by dropping backwards onto the mat in order to throw your opponent. I find it hard to pluck up the courage to try *tomoe-nage* in a contest, and many players hate being thrown by it. But give it a go, as they say in Wellington. (Well, they say 'Kill him!' actually.) I did once use it at a grading, as we have seen — albeit in a slow and ladylike way — but it isn't part of my normal repertoire.

The British Judo Association syllabus offers its customary accurate, yet curiously baffling, description of this throw. You have to clutch your opponent's lapels with both hands, stick your foot in their stomach and straighten your leg as you sit down and fall backwards, thus sending the other player over your head onto their back. Or, as my *Kodokan Judo* book rather thrillingly promises: 'Your opponent will fly over your head and land on the mat some distance from you.' It is probably worth stressing again that you must be careful throwing a bloke with this technique, or you will inadvertently give him something to think about.[1]

The time to attempt this throw is when your opponent is pushing you away with straight arms, and you can't get in close enough for your usual techniques. Stiff-arming is common with novices. When someone is trying to attack you, holding them

---

[1] Such as, how wise women are to wear their reproductive gear safely on the inside.

off in rigid terror feels like the obvious thing to do. Once you have been *tomoe-nagi*-ed a couple of times, you are alert to the risk. The minute someone takes a double-lapel grip, you know what's coming. In fact, you can generally stop your opponent stiff-arming by raising a foot and feinting a *tomoe-nage* without having to go through with it. If you are good at judo you will then follow up the feint with a different throw and win the bout. Rather than, say, falling about laughing, which is my normal follow-up technique.

Personally, I find it difficult to get past the feeling that *tomoe-nage* is a bit unsporting,[1] a bit, you know, *mean*. I have a problem with meanness. It's one of the epithets I would least like people to apply to me, and I hate being on the receiving end, too. I dare say my attitude to *tomoe-nage* is just a symptom of a more serious malaise picked up in church: chronic wimpiness. 'Whatever you wish that men would do to you, do so to them; for this is the law and the prophets' (Matthew, 7:12). This potentially puts a large conceptual spanner in the judo works. So do the words of Jesus: 'If anyone strikes you on the right

----

[1] Interestingly, my American spellchecker doesn't recognise this word.

cheek, turn to him the other also.'[1]

But to return to *tomoe-nage*. I'm probably just being a twit. It's a perfectly respectable throw, enshrined in the British Judo Association syllabus, and I need to get over my squeamishness. No, I wouldn't want someone to do it to me, but then, I don't want them to execute *any* successful technique on me in a contest. It's not nice to be *tomoe*-ed, because you feel like you are diving head first onto the mat and are about to break your neck. If you remember to tuck and roll, you should be fine. Try not to stick your hands out, unless you are very gymnastic and can do a handspring, or can cartwheel out of the technique and land on your feet.

If you are intending to use a sacrifice technique, you must commit yourself whole-heartedly. Just give it a go, 100 per cent, like the psychopathic Kiwi you secretly want to be. If you don't, there's a chance an inattentive ref will see you on your back and infer that you've been thrown there by your

---

[1] This may not be as doormatty as it sounds. Given that most people are right-handed, a blow to the right cheek is going to be a contemptuous back handed flick. Offering your left cheek becomes a challenge, a way of saying, Do that again, and this time do it properly.

opponent. There's an even bigger chance your opponent will dive on top of you and pin you down. The way to counter a right-footed *tomoe-nage* is to step swiftly out of the way to your left, while pushing your opponent's raised foot to the right. This means they are on their back and you are deemed to have contributed to the technique, therefore you should be given a score. However, you might not, it depends on the ref, so make sure you land on them and get some kind of hold on. But not in a mean way.

Diary

12 September 2005

September always feels like the beginning of a new year to me. Years of being locked into the academic calendar, I suppose. The air is fraught with anticipation and possibility. January feels a bit arbitrary in comparison. This is the time for taking up new challenges, making new resolutions, or at least revamping the old ones. I've been going out running on and off over the summer, but now that the new school term has started, I'm trying to be more disciplined about it. Judo at the Wolverhampton Club starts again this week. Oak Park (or Bloke Park, as our younger son calls it) Judo Club has been going on over the summer, apart from the bank holiday weekend, when we were turfed out of the big sports hall for a rabbit show. I've only been managing the odd training session here and there, which is always bad news, since it means you are repeatedly going through the first session agony barrier of aching neck and shoulders, wrenched muscles and joints, without ever toughening up fully.

Pete and I went running while we were on holiday in Brittany. The terrain was mercifully flat. We stayed on little country lanes through maize fields and past apple trees dropping their windfalls into little ditches. Back home we have carried on. We do a three-and-a-bit-mile loop through the arboretum extension up to the canal, along the towpath back to the main road, then home again. The last time we went Pete had given blood a couple of hours previously, so for once he was slowing me down. (He seems genuinely to believe that a pint of blood regenerates itself in about forty-five minutes if you concentrate.) He's B-negative, so they were pretty keen to get his donation, although he's been bounced repeat-edly for having grown up in India. They are worried about malaria. This being his first time for a while, he had to go through the full screening process. Have you had anal sex with a man? Have you taken drugs? Have you had sex with a drug user? Have you had sex with someone who has had anal sex with a drug user? Have you had sex in Africa? Have you had hepatitis? Have you ever sold your body for sex? Have you stood in a crowded port and shouted, Hello, sailor? After a while Pete said he wanted to cry, 'I protest! The tendency of this line of questioning is to make me look completely square! I don't like saying 'No'. I'm a very positive person and I like saying 'Yes' '. Have you been abroad in the last twelve months? YES! Yes, I *have*! I've been to France *and* Italy *and* Spain! he sobbed in relief. Have you been to the dentist recently? YES!! ONLY LAST WEEK!

Funnily enough, the run was just a second outside our second fastest time (according to Pete, who likes to make a note of these things so that he can at least compete against himself, even if he's the only one running). I'd love to tell you how fast that is, but I don't do numbers and figures. I couldn't tell you offhand what our car registration is, although I generally recognise the car when I see it. It's black. I still know the number of the Austin my dad had in the early seventies, mind you — MNK 855D. Short-term memory loss is a bugger. I bet it's caused by my brain being clogged up with useless trivia. A bit like a computer with a full memory. Wouldn't it be good to be able to delete stuff and make room for things like your National Insurance number, and whatever it was you went into the kitchen for? *Are you sure you want to permanently delete the file 'Donny Osmond's birthday'?* your screen would ask.

When I run my only challenge is to get round my course without stopping or taking short cuts. Pete, of course, runs with a stopwatch, which he checks at various points along the route and tells me things like we are twelve seconds behind our third best time since coming back from France. Still, it's paying off, I think. I do run harder when I'm with him. This isn't because he bullies me. He just runs beside me at my pace, without criticism, just offering encouragement by his companionship. On hot days he carries a water bottle and hands it to me when I'm gasping. Once I fumbled the handover. We dropped a couple of seconds there, I'm afraid.

On Saturday I was out running and saw the woman whose dog bit me. We greeted one another cheerily. She had a new dog. It was a lot smaller and didn't bark at me. I still gave it a wide berth. Rather than stomping on it as I passed. Oh! Well, I've never done *that* before! A couple of weeks after the biting incident Pete was taking a funeral. A man approached him when the service was over and said, 'Your wife was bitten by a dog, wasn't she?' 'Yes, she was.' 'That's ever so sad,' the man said shaking his head. Pete was surprised and touched by his concern, until he went on, 'The dog had to be put down, you know.'

26 September 2005
Went for my longer run this morning and it felt

good after a week of struggling with a cold and with various muscle pulls. I keep twanging my hamstring, and then on Thursday at judo I pulled my quads while working on a new technique, *yoko otoshi*, a sacrifice throw that I think I could find a use for. Maybe I need to warm up differently, or better. It has crossed my mind that this is a sign of ageing. When I was a child I could sprint without any warm-up, and never suffer for it. Perhaps the problem is that I don't allow enough recovery time when I've pulled something. I think that a nice gentle jog will loosen things up. This is a pernicious piece of nonsense I've learned from Pete, who acts as if you can run off bubonic plague. This is what I did on Friday morning — ran round the block to help my quad injury. On Saturday I could barely walk down the stairs without going Aargh! on alternate steps. Still, next grading isn't until 13 November, so I've got plenty of time to recover.

6

Brown Belt

Cast care aside, lean on thy guide;
His boundless mercy will provide;
Trust, and thy trusting soul shall prove
Christ is its life, and Christ its love.

Verse 3, Hymn 54, 'Fight the Good Fight'

in *With Cheerful Voice: Hymns for Children*

This is the chapter about where it all went wrong.

Suddenly that sentence worries me. In another few months I may look back and laugh like the lost soul of a hyena. Who's to say how much more hideously wronger they could go? But come now! 'Cast care aside, lean on thy guide,' as the hymn admonishes us. While I am singing these words I am able to banish that nagging little question:

Why Am I Doing This?

When I got back from New Zealand my drive seemed to evaporate. Yes, I still enjoyed judo: turning up for training, having a good laugh with my mates. I just wasn't sure about the whole grading aspect. When the next one came along, I whinged about not wanting to go, and Keith said, 'Well, don't then.' Perhaps this was supposed to brace me up, to make me think, then redouble my efforts. Or maybe he was just fed up with me moaning. Whatever he intended, I took it as permission not to go. After all, I 'didn't feel ready'.

Not feeling ready is a useful sporting concept. It implies something thought-out and serious. It suggests that you have been monitoring the progress of your training, listening to your body and, after careful consideration, you have concluded that more preparation is needed at this stage. In my case, it was simply a loss of nerve. Three months in a club where they could (and did) all massacre me, undermined my confidence in my fighting skills.

I skipped the first grading, and then didn't feel ready for the one after that, either. When the next one came along, I was ill. Sort of. Anyway, it clashed with an important church service I told myself I oughtn't to miss. The urgency seeped out of my ambition to get a black belt. I'd started by telling myself I'd do it by the time I was forty-five, and that had seemed like an overgenerous margin. I'd do it *way* before then, easy-peasy. By the autumn of 2003 I began thinking, well, I've still got three years, so there's no pressure.

Then came the New Year, with the annual life audit and steely resolutions. Looking back at my journal, I see that I set myself a few targets: 'to get my 1st kyu [top brown belt] and do my black-belt theory and to get another novel accepted'. By the end of the year I had scored a fat zero out of 3, but my heart was in the right place — 2004 would be different.

It was, but in ways I hadn't anticipated. After four years of alternately trying and *not* trying (in the sense of pretending not to be trying), I discovered in March that I was pregnant. After all those months of raised and dashed hopes, my first thought on seeing the little blue line was, *Oh bloody hell, what have I done?* When I rang my husband at work with the happy news, I burst into tears, and I'm afraid they weren't tears of joy. I clung onto the idea that I *would* be happy. Of course I would! It would be fine! I managed to pin a trembly smile on my face. It lasted until I was assailed by an image of me pushing the buggy through Walsall's arboretum in a year's time and people saying, 'Grandchildren are such a joy, aren't they?'

I knew why I was so anxious. Four years earlier I had thought I was expecting, only to discover something had gone wrong at conception. I wasn't genuinely pregnant at all, despite my body being so awash with hormones that I was unable to eat for nausea. My assumption has always been that hypochondria automatically exempts you from having any serious or interesting medical condition. I had never heard of molar pregnancies. I'd gone up to the hospital at ten weeks for a scan which was intended merely to set my mind at rest. I found myself caught up in a flurry of medical activity and booked in for an evacuation at once.

It was Holy Week. I was on my own at hospital. Pete was running a children's holiday club down at church and I couldn't get hold of him. One of the nurses rang a good friend of mine, Pat, who is a midwife. She came and sat with me as I waited for more scans and tests. At about four I managed to get hold of Pete and sob the truth out on the phone. He arrived as I was being prepared for theatre. I had never had an operation before and was terrified. Then a registrar appeared and announced in a breezy doctorish way, 'Oh, we've decided you can go home for the night. We're postponing your procedure till tomorrow. We need everyone on hand because of the risk of bleeding. Sleep well!'

She didn't actually say the last bit, and needless to say, I didn't sleep well. It did give us the chance to Google 'molar pregnancy', though, and scare ourselves further. The following morning I was lying on a noisy ward, waiting, tears leaking in a steady stream onto my waterproof pillow, hearing the woman on the far bed repeating her symptoms to anyone who passed, like a news bulletin on a loop ('If it wasn't for my catheter I'd be home now, the consultant says'). It was Good Friday. I wanted it to be over, but I dreaded the anaesthetic. What if I died? As I was wheeled down for surgery I saw a yellow elephant painted on the theatre doors. I remember thinking, *I'm going to die, and the last thing I'll see on this earth is a bloody yellow elephant.*

I came round sobbing. They wheeled me back to the ward and there was Pete. OK. I wasn't dead, then. As I lay still seeping tears, I gradually realised that I no longer felt sick, that I was hungry, that — implausibly — I felt physically better than I had for weeks and weeks. They let me go home in the afternoon, and I left wishing with all my soul never to be back on that obs & gynae ward ever again.

Months of blood and urine tests followed, and scary letters from Charing Cross Hospital stamped ONCOLOGY DEPART-MENT. We were told not to try for another baby until I was given the all-clear. While the chances of a molar pregnancy occurring in the first place are tiny, the odds of it happening a second time were hugely increased. In the event, I was signed off after six months. Everything was fine — apart from our apparent inability to conceive.

All my fears rushed back when I finally saw that little blue line four years later. Until I'd had a scan, we couldn't be sure that the problem hadn't recurred. The wait was anguished. I was scanned at seven weeks and they told us at once that all was well — definitely not molar, definitely not twins. We saw the foetal heartbeat. I remember walking away from the hospital back to the car and saying to Pete, 'So it's really going to happen, then.' But at some level — despite the sickness and exhaustion, the looking at pretty nursery fabrics in John Lewis and kicking myself for getting rid of the car seat — I never totally, totally believed in it. It could all still go wrong.

My plan was to carry on doing some gentle judo training. No heavy falls, of course. Keith had other ideas: 'DEFINITELY NO FIGHT-ING (or lifting heavy objects like mats or us), you madwoman.' Or words to that effect. Ah, no *lifting*! Yes, I'd forgotten about that, I thought. There was a whole lot I'd forgotten during the decade that had elapsed since I was last expecting a baby; most strikingly, that I wouldn't feel like getting off the sofa, let alone into my judo kit and onto the mat.

As the weeks went by I gradually got the hang of pregnancy again. Those grandmother fears grew less acute. After all, plenty of women far older than me had babies all the time. I began to think the idea might bear my weight if trod cautiously. Yes, it was daft. Before long I'd have a fourteen-year-old, a twelve-year-old and a one-year-old, but so what? It was wonderful, too. We reached the magical twelve-week mark and told everyone. Our sons were beside themselves with delight, desperate to get off to school and tell all their friends.

The following morning I miscarried. Pat, my midwife friend, was off work, and she came with me and Pete to the hospital. There I was, back on the obs & gynae ward, nil by mouth for twenty-four hours while I was repeatedly promised that I was next on the list, if only they could get an anaesthetist, and there weren't any real emergencies. Whenever I sat up I passed out from blood loss. My head rang and jangled with a million microscopic alarm bells and chainsaws. I had a cannula for a drip in the crook of my elbow because the veins in my hand had collapsed from low blood pressure. It ached and seeped blood and there was no comfortable position to lie in. Dimly, a voice kept enquiring in my head, *Who would have thought the old woman had so much blood in her?* Bag after bag of saline solution dripped into my arm.

All through that day and night a parade of anaesthetists presented themselves to me, asked me if I had false teeth or implants, and promised to take care of me, only to vanish from my life forever. At about 4 a.m. a dark good-looking Frenchman appeared at my bedside saying, 'Catereen, I am 'ere to take care of you.' I was assured later that there is no such person at the Manor Hospital. If I were a Christian of a different type, I might conclude it was an angel, albeit a Mills & Boon one. Over and over I heard sirens approaching in the dark, and every time I wept in despair to think I was being shunted down the rota once more. Then I wept because I was being selfish. Then I wept again because I didn't *care* if I was selfish, I just wanted it over and done with. I was starving. My head hurt. I couldn't sleep. The oddest thing was that behind it all, underneath it all, I sensed kindness. That somehow it was all fine. And even if I were to die, then that too, somehow, would be . . . all right.

In the morning another friend, Mandy, came to see me from the maternity wing. She was booked in for a Caesarean section that same day. We had been planning to push our buggies together round the arboretum. This was the second time we'd planned that. Four years before she had sat and wept with me for my loss while she was eight months pregnant herself. It became a strange companionship, oddly desolate, when her own desperately longed-for daughter Eleanor died aged two weeks in the same hospital. So of course she came to see me, just as I stumbled across to Maternity that afternoon to meet her baby boy. What else would either of us do? Where else would we be other than with a dear friend, whether it's to share sorrow or to share joy? Some things are denied us in this life. We never will get to do the buggy-pushing together. But even now it seems to me that the last word is kindness; the kindness of God underneath it all, and the kindness of good friends.

The kindness of strangers and slight

acquaintances is harder to bear, however. After Mandy had gone I had a visit from a chaplaincy volunteer, and it was like being assaulted by a Joyce Grenfell monologue. 'Ooh! Nil by mouth! *That* doesn't sound very good! So! What's the matter, then?' Years of practice (and if I'm honest, the inhibiting presence of my husband by the bed) restrained me from shouting, 'Just *fuck* off!' Instead I sobbed that I didn't want to talk about it, but she nevertheless lingered for several more minutes, apologising and patting my leg and explaining that she didn't wish to intrude, but that many patients loved to talk, and didn't she recognise my husband from somewhere? 'Hmm,' he said, after she'd finally gone. 'A *little* more basic training, perhaps.'

Afterwards, when it was all over and I was home again, there was so much emptiness to be endured. Empty womb, empty arms. Acres of empty grief to slog through. Miscarriages are so common that it amazes me how much it matters and for how long. Even when you think you've got over it, you discover that your subconscious has been keeping its own diary of little anniversaries — the due date, a year on from conception, the first birthday. Waves of grief engulf you on seemingly calm days.

For me the emptiness was like a ferocious presence at first. It woke me in panic at 3 a.m. with nightmares of starving pets in the attic which I had inexplicably neglected. My resurrected maternal anxieties latched on to my sons, as if they were babies again and needed me round the clock. All I found to pour my energies into was their diet. No more junk food. Only home-made cakes and bread. No crisp to pass the threshold ever again. They bore it well. Now and then they would improvise a skit based on Neo dodging bullets in slow motion in *The Matrix*. Beware the full blast of Mum's worry! Whoa! It can strip the flesh off your bones!

For many weeks the anguish was so acute I felt as if I was walking around with a hatchet buried in my sternum. Occasionally I would glance down and rub my breastbone, amazed there was no handle jutting out. No wonder they talk of broken hearts. Grief is imperious. It has its whims and tyrannies. Sometimes I wanted to talk, sometimes I didn't. Some people were permitted to approach, others were not. I made a mental note never to say to another woman, 'If it's any comfort, I had a miscarriage myself once.' Because no, frankly, it's no comfort at all. It is supremely irrelevant. Just as, in some inadmissible way, it feels irrelevant that 'at least I have two lovely sons'.

On my first Sunday back at church I sat with Mandy and her new baby. We'd been somewhere like this before. There had been one perfect June day, four years before, when we'd sat in a rose garden and watched the dragonflies flickering over a pond, and heard the stock doves brooding overhead in the trees. I said, 'This is as good as it gets.' The moment was miraculously suspended in that waste of grief, shining and complete, like a bead of rain on a lupin leaf. When I try to explain this to other people, they look shocked.

I felt like a failure. I still do, if I let myself dwell on it. It was an awful year. In January Pete was caught up in an employment tribunal which we knew might drag on for the whole twelve months. Well, I told myself when the first wave of legal acrimony was unleashed, at least 2004 will also be the year our third child was born. We'll have something glorious to put all the rubbish and vitriol into perspective. But the one thing I most wanted to be able to do for my beloved, I failed in. And I failed to give my sons their baby brother or sister. Of course, if I heard anyone else saying this kind of thing about themselves, I'd protest. It's not failure! Don't be ridiculous. You can't blame yourself, it's not your fault. I know. I *know*. I don't blame myself, but still, I set out on a mission and my body simply couldn't finish it. Where do you go from there?

Everything passes. It passes, then it fades. Gradually the first racking pain eased. The hatchet dropped out somewhere along the path. In a funny way I missed it. After an extreme emotional state, normality feels flat, like the aftermath of a hurricane. The drama is over. Now you have to start dealing with the debris and wreckage. The task is overwhelming. People sometimes describe depression as a black dog. But at least a dog is company, I found myself thinking. It follows you around the place. Grief leaves a gap when it goes, even if you'd never wish yourself back under its shadow.

And so a different kind of emptiness followed, more an aimlessness. It was like emerging after a heartbreaking climb up to a plateau only to find yourself looking out over a desert. It was a desert of free time and space I hadn't expected to enjoy for years. Now what am I going to do? What's the point of me? It takes a while to gather up the threads you've dropped. I threw myself into things with a panicked drivenness. I went back to judo, but it was too soon. We were only doing practice throws on the soft crash mat, but I simply couldn't take it. 'I'm going to have to go home,' I told Keith. He looked at me very kindly and said he just wanted to give me a hug. 'Don't! Don't be nice to me, I'll only cry.' (He and Debbie both offered to punch me instead.)

I sat in the car sobbing until finally I could see straight enough to drive home. What's the *matter* with me? I wept. It turned out that I was anaemic, which I suppose should have been obvious. But that was only part of it. There is something about the judo mat that brings the emotions up to the surface for me. It forces me to acknowledge how closely the physical and the psychological are knitted together. In a way, the mental *is* physical: the human brain is blood and meat, chemistry and physics. I may have an abstract ideal of myself that is strong and tough, but the dojo finds me out every time. There's no hiding. Back then I was weak. I was broken and grieving. So I had to go home and give myself time to mend and find out what I really wanted, now that my hopes had been dashed. I needed to rebuild my body and grow some more red blood cells. I needed to be kind to me.

★ ★ ★

Gradually, over the course of the summer, my strength came back. But it was hard to be patient. A friend of mine had a transfusion after childbirth. She told me she could see why people referred to 'life blood', because she could literally feel the strength pouring in through her arm. That would have been nice. It takes a lot longer with iron tablets. There was a small hill that led back up onto the far end of our road and later on whenever I ran up it I thought, This is the place where I had to stop and walk when I was anaemic. It reminded me not to take my physical well-being for granted.

I pondered strength and weakness a lot that summer. Why does it matter so much to me to be strong, and never to cry on the mat? Am I still a ten-year-old, fiercely and futilely trying to be one of the boys? Why do I so desperately want to be tough? I sensed an answer in myself: if I'm tough and strong, nothing can hurt me. I will be armoured against attack. I will be impervious.

One of the toughest men I've known was Neil, of course. He was a judo and ju-jitsu black belt and I used to train with him on Saturdays. He was in the Territorial Army and fought in Iraq. Then he was knocked down and killed by a speeding car. Toughness is no guarantee. I still half look for him every

Saturday afternoon. I picture him coming in to the sports hall and rolling his eyes at us all for being daft enough to think he was gone for good. Now and then he flashes into my mind when I'm standing on one leg clutching my other ankle and stretching my quad muscles. Occasionally he'd wait until I'd got my balance, then push me over. When I got up indignantly, he'd be staring off into space with Zen-like calm, balancing on one leg as if nothing had happened.

My need to be tough was part of the same panicked obsession that had me baking bread and cookies. It was an unspoken attempt to atone for the times when I'd been weak and failed to protect the ones who depended on me. My spiritual director challenged me to accept that the worst had happened. My baby had died. There was nothing I could have done to prevent it, nothing I could do now, or needed to do, to atone. 'It is finished,' she told me.

The Bible has a lot to say about strength and weakness. Much of it is paradoxical: 'My [i.e. God's] grace is sufficient for you. My strength is made perfect in weakness.' 'When I am weak, then I am strong.'[1] The idea of

_____

[1] My mother once saw a typo which read, 'When I am weak, then am I string.'

231

weakness as strength is enshrined in martial arts, too, and often expressed in the cherry tree/willow tree analogy. The wind blows and the stronger branches of the cherry break, while the weak and supple willow branches bend and survive the storm. This is the gentle way: yielding in order to defeat a stronger opponent by exploiting the opponent's own strength and weight. I find the idea attractive. See, I am supple and wily, I go with the flow, I exploit adversity to my own ends. Contrary to appearances, I am actually in control.

I wish. As a good evangelical, I assume that Jesus is the template of Christian strength. This is less reassuring than the willow tree school of thought. I see Jesus sweating blood in Gethsemane. He goes on to face his trial and death steadily and with courage and dignity. But on the brink of death when he cries out on the cross, 'My God, my God, why hast thou forsaken me?' I have to conclude he felt he'd failed. He hadn't foreseen the terrible abandonment.

I have an image of a bungee jump down into the deepest abyss. You stand looking down. An empty wind whistles around you. It is dark. All you can hear is your own blood thrashing in your ears. This is not good, you think. There doesn't appear to be a bottom. But all shall be well and all manner of thing shall be well. Surely? The moment comes. They count you down. You summon your nerve and dive. The elastic spools out behind you as you fall. Down, down, down into the blackness. At what point do you finally grasp that the other end of the elastic is not attached?

The problem with evangelicals is that we are basically inclined to Docetism, that ancient heresy which said that Jesus only *seemed* to be human, but he wasn't actually, he was all divine. If Jesus was God, the evangelical reasoning goes, he was omniscient. He could have passed GCSE French and invented the mobile phone if he'd felt like it. Therefore he knew it was all OK, that once he'd got the cross over with, he'd be coming back. When he said, 'Why hast thou forsaken me?' he was just quoting Psalm 22, because it felt rather like he'd been forsaken, although he knew he hadn't been really. Docetism leaves no room for that moment of sheer horror when the end of the bungee rope went snaking past his ear and he realised his God had dropped him down the bottomless abyss.

Once in a while, when I wonder what God is really like, I read some Karl Barth. In the world of theology, this is a minority sport. It's a bit like thinking, I'm thirsty, and taking your tumbler to the Niagara Falls. Barth's vision of God comes crashing over you until you are battered half unconscious. I find this a useful corrective to the evangelical vision of Jesus as my boyfriend. 'HE IS THE HIDDEN ABYSS!' thunders Barth. Fortunately, he goes on to add, 'He is also the hidden home at the beginning and the end of all our journeyings.'

I am gradually accepting that I'm neither expected nor required to be strong. I remember sobbing and pleading all the way to Wolverhampton once during that horrible autumn as I drove to judo: 'I just want to be strong again, please let me be strong!' Predictably, no Teflon mind and body armour was forthcoming. Strength of a new kind comes in the admission of being weak. Sometimes it takes more courage to give in than to carry on striving and shoring up your defences.

Eventually I saw that I'd set myself an impossible task. It was like trying single-handedly to maintain a vast medieval castle, frantically mending the walls, patrolling the parapets, manning the drawbridge. I suddenly saw that it was a ruin. Then it dawned on me that in its own way it was beautiful, with the sunlight on the old crumbling stone, and the spring flowers starting to come up. I could lie back on the grassy mound and look up at the sky. Give over, just give over. Let it fall down if it wants to. Don't be scared. If people come, they are probably just visitors, rather than enemies. For all you know, they might wish you well. You don't necessarily have to drop boiling oil on them.

So. It was a relief to admit I was weak. I didn't have to pick up where I left off and fight at the same level. It was OK to be too feeble to apply an effective strangle, or to get exhausted after thirty seconds of *randori*. I let myself listen to Keith, and take it steady. There was only one person making impossible demands, and that was me. And finally I began to do what Kano had been telling me all along: give way.

★ ★ ★

That was my Damascus Road moment. Everything clicked into place and my judo instantly improved beyond all recognition and I got a black belt! With which I shall now ceremonially throttle myself for telling fibs. No, there have been no Damascene moments on this journey. Now and then a small light bulb goes on — like when Debbie suggests an adjustment to some throw I've always been crap at, and suddenly it works. Mostly I am only aware of improvement when I look back and see how far I've come.

By the time you reach brown belt you've come quite a long way. You will have proved yourself adept at more than twenty throws for your licence, to say nothing of armlocks, holds, escapes, strangles and judo-related Japanese. My favourite throw is a brown-belt technique: *sasae-tsuri-komi-ashi*. The BJA syllabus translates this inscrutably as 'propping drawing angle'. *Kodokan Judo* is slightly more forthcoming with 'supporting foot lift-pull throw'. Whatever. Come round and I'll show you. The next throw in the syllabus is *harai-tsuri-komi-ashi* ('sweeping drawing ankle'). 'This may look very similar to the previous throw,' chides the BJA, 'but there is a big difference.'[1]

Since taking up the sport again, I have been a keen evangelist for judo. 'Come to judo!' I say, seizing someone by the lapels. 'You'll love it.' Misreading their body language (I assume they are trying to run straight to the club and enrol), I grip them and rant on and on, offering to pick them up and drive them to the dojo, or even buy them a *judogi*. Occasionally I extract some kind of

---

[1] Presumably because you attack the ankle, not the angle.

promise from my victim, and am amazed afresh each week when they never show up. 'But they said they were coming!' My clubmates pull my leg about my imaginary friends. (We try not to evangelise like this for the church, incidentally. We aim for sensitivity, especially if, like my husband, we shave our heads and are sometimes mistaken for a nightclub bouncer.[1]

When I stop to think about it, I am capable of admitting that judo might be a bit on the . . . well, violent side for some people. I'm afraid judo is a shock to the system if, in the normal routines of your daily life, you aren't much in the habit of flinging yourself about and landing hard on the floor. During your very first session you may be deposited gently in a caring way onto a padded crash mat. Even so, it can be a bit traumatic.

Those days are a distant memory to me now because I've toughened up. Maybe my pain threshold is higher. Or maybe it's a question of attitude, and I don't count certain

---

[1] 'You're never a vicar!' he was told in a pub once. 'You look well hard. *I'd* come to church if you told me to.' 'Actually, that's what I do,' Pete replied. 'I stand outside on Sunday morning going 'Oi! You! Get in here NOW!' '

things as pain (landing on the mat, say), because they are simply a normal part of my sport. Rather like being in labour. According to folk wisdom and natural-childbirth manuals, it isn't actually pain, as such. It just *feels* like pain to the unenlightened woman going through it. I am forever hurting my toes on the mat, twisting and wrenching them as I go for foot sweeps. I hop about cursing, but I'm sure I recover much more quickly than I would have done in my pre-judo existence, if I'd stubbed my toe in the dark against a bed leg.

Judo has definitely taught me a different attitude to pain. While we don't actively seek them out, injuries have a certain kudos. This has created a special etiquette: a combination of taking pain seriously, while simultaneously shrugging it off. This is why I always refer to my 'foot injury', not my 'poorly toe'. If someone asks about it, I know I'm not supposed to whinge. I'm supposed to say lightly that it's fine, but limp a bit at the earliest opportunity to display my fortitude.

My foot injury is actually arthritis in my right big toe joint, I'm sorry to say. I've had it checked out officially, X-rayed and so forth, and the podiatrist says it's arthritis. It isn't caused by wearing ridiculous 'True Love

Waits' shoes,[1] which is extremely annoying, as my mother promised me every time she forced me into a new pair of Clarks lace-ups, that I'd thank her when I was forty and still had nice feet. It's because my metatarsal is too long, apparently, a hereditary fault handed on by my father who suffers from the same problem (and, as far as I am aware, has never worn stilettos in his life). 'What can I do about it?' I asked the consultant. 'We can shorten the bone for you,' he replied, 'and open the joint up and clean it out.' He prophesied that I would need this done if I wanted to carry on doing judo, so naturally I went away and never returned, staving off surgery by a combination of cod liver oil and denial.[2] So far I've been OK, although there are a couple of things I can't do, such as squat thrusts or walking more than twenty yards in killer heels. I've had to adapt some of my judo techniques so as not to put pressure on the damaged joint, and now and then I

---

[1] Evangelicals aren't allowed to wear fuck-me shoes.

[2] This is the pure martial-arts response to illness and injury. If your leg drops off, put Tiger Balm on the stump — rather that than fall into the dubious clutches of the medical profession, who only ever prescribe drugs.

accidentally boot someone, which is excruciating. For me, I mean. Who cares about them? If they don't want to get hurt, they can go and do t'ai chi.

There is also the vexed question of whether women and men have different pain thresholds. Are men all big babies, as many women like to claim? When I was new to judo I once listened in on a conversation between Keith and some of the other blokes as they compared major injuries. These consisted mainly of broken limbs and welding accidents. 'What about you?' they asked. 'Well, I've given birth twice,' I said. This is a good gambit. No bloke is going to risk saying, 'Pff! that's nothing!' My observation is that when it comes to pain, some blokes are drama queens, others are silent stoics. The same applies to women. I'm a drama queen but an aspiring stoic.

Judo is a rough old sport. People do get hurt. Usually these injuries are minor. Mat burns are common.[1] Fingernails get ripped. This is why I always bite mine short. The tiny blonde in Wellington had nice nails. I asked

---

[1] This is where you zip the top of your foot across the floor and lose the top layers of skin. Your socks will then stick to the weeping wound, which is obscurely satisfying.

her before the session if she was going to cut them, and she said no. Later on I heard, as I'd known I would, one of the cauliflower-eared men warble out in tones of mincing fayness, 'Oh, *stop*, everyone! Hannah's broken a *nail*!' Julie, who started coming to our club a few months ago, is still valiantly holding out. 'I live in a world where women have long hair and nice nails,' she lamented. 'Where women are *feminine*.' Debbie, Heather and I exchanged butch sneers (before hiding our hands up our sleeves).

Bumps and bruises are par for the course. I've been dumped on my face on the mat — it hurt like hell, but even as I bit back the tears a sneaky thought went through my mind that this was going to look pretty impressive the next morning. Disappointingly, the resulting friction burn looked like an allergy, as if I'd reacted badly to a new moisturiser.

In fact, all my best facial injuries have ended up looking like cosmetics-related blunders. I had high hopes of the one genuine shiner I got just before Christmas a couple of years ago. I was immensely satisfied with it, as proud as if I'd plucked up courage to shave my head or get a tattoo. However, the next day it merely looked as though I'd made one eye up with vivid purple eyeshadow and, like an idiot, forgotten the other. I was easily outclassed by a woman in her seventies who'd tripped on her garden path and landed face first. The curate suggested we sat next to one another in church so people would think we'd had a punch-up. I declined, fearing they'd actually conclude I'd duffed up a defenceless old lady, who had nonetheless gamely managed to land a punishing right hook. Lots of people commented. More worrying were the people who noticed, but looked away and said nothing. Well, he seems like a nice man, that vicar, but you never can tell, can you?

More serious injuries are, of course, a real possibility, but they are pretty rare, I'm glad to say. Care is taken by the British Judo Association to ban any technique that seems to be resulting in a lot of injuries, especially to the neck. In the time I've been doing judo, there has been a broken collarbone, a broken ankle and a dislocated kneecap in our club. Oh, and a few broken ribs and toes. Jo, who shared the same ambition as her twin sister Heather to reach dan grade and become a judo coach, took a nasty fall at a grading a couple of years back and broke her elbow. She hasn't regained full mobility in the joint, and will probably never do judo again. She seems resigned, and is now doing a degree in forensic science instead.

Predictably — because the stakes are higher and the fighting tougher — the worst accident I've witnessed took place at a grading. It was a broken arm and it was the only occasion I've heard a man scream; not a manly yelp, but a real falsetto screaming, 'Jesus fucking Christ!' echoing round the cavernous sports hall. (Mostly the blokes just go, 'Foo! Hah!' when injured, as though eating a rather too hot vindaloo.) I think the screaming shamed and chilled us all. I found myself thinking, What if that were my husband? One of my (male) clubmates said callously, 'Well, he obviously didn't warm up properly.'

No amount of stretching will protect you from that freak awkward fall, of course. The idea is that it may help prevent muscle tears and pulled ligaments. But infinitely more important than any hamstring stretch is the use of Proper Equipment. Tons of it. Or so I conclude from the array of knee braces and strapping some of the men sport. A disloyal spy from the men's changing room — let's call him Gary (because that's his name) — told me it's a bit like watching medieval knights armouring up for a jousting match. Most of these contraptions fasten with Velcro, so you can draw attention to your injury by readjusting your strapping now and then with mighty ripping sounds while denying that it hurts. And bandaged knuckles: a good look. We like it. Even if you're not bleeding, tape 'em up. It gives off a well-hard vibe. In the past I have occasionally strapped my little toe to its neighbour with micropore tape to prevent it being wrenched out of joint yet again. Lloyd from the Saturday club sticks his toes up *with electrical tape*. But he's got his black belt. I wouldn't presume to do that yet.

There have been times when I've sat in church on Sunday mornings aching from head to foot. My neck and shoulders are so stiff and sore that I can almost feel tears welling up. I could take painkillers, but I don't. There's something meet and right about the pain. Foo! Hah! It feels *good*. I worked to get it. I'm tough enough to take it. I will mount up on wings like an eagle, I will run and not be weary, I will walk and not grow faint. I may occasionally stay sitting down in the hymns, though.

Diary

12 October 2005

A month till the next grading, and I'm already anxious. There's too much emptiness in my life and worries grow to fill the space available. I went for a three-mile run this morning thinking it would lift my mood, but came back as full of miseries as ever. Sometimes it feels like an attack of grief, like an attack of guilt, or panic; something almost physical in its intensity. I'm still not over that miscarriage, and the empty place where I'd thought another child would be. I catch myself thinking, I shouldn't be feeling this, I have a nice life. But the fact is I *am* feeling it. I need to find ways to cope. Strategies for life.

The hard thing is that judo and this sorrow are filed under the same heading at the moment. Judo used to be in a folder with 'Fun!' Now it's got muddled up with guilt, anxiety and sorrow. This is why I can't face the grading blithely with the thought that it's nothing. I can't tell myself, Just give it a go, see if you can pick up some more points; if not, no big deal. It has become a very big deal indeed. If I had something real to worry about, gradings would be nothing. However, I'd really rather *not* have something real to worry about, any more than a hypochondriac wants cancer. Although a tiny part of them secretly thinks it would be a relief. See? I was right. At last, a focus for my anxiety! If they don't secretly think this, they probably don't have *real* hypochondria, they're just imagining it.

15 November 2005
It's two days after the grading, and once again I got no points. I had four fights and lost them all. I chose not to write a pre-grading diary entry, as my preparation strategy involved doing nothing that would make me feel worse about it, and lots of things to make me feel better. Writing it all down comes very high up the list of things that makes me feel worse.

So this is why I didn't sit up here in my study on Saturday night nothing down exactly how I was feeling. I wouldn't have slept. Instead, I went to a Gospel concert down at church, which occupied my time and cheered my soul. I slept reasonably well, and arrived at the new judo centre feeling much better than I'd feared I would.
My other very cunning strategy, one suggested

by Keith and Debbie, was that I did my dan-grade theory on the same day. This meant lots of mugging up of the Gokyo — a collection of throws and armlocks, strangles and pin-downs — in order to be able to demonstrate them on demand to the examiner. I practised with Heather, who kindly agreed to be my *uke* on the day. In the week running up to the grading I kept waking at 3 a.m. in a cold sweat thinking, *Kata gatame!* What's *kata gatame?* But by Sunday morning I'd got most of it lodged in my memory. There were a couple of techniques I knew, but couldn't execute very well. The worst was my old nemesis *kata-garuma*, the fireman's lift followed by flipping your partner over onto the mat. Either I collapse under my partner's weight, or I injure my back. Yes, yes, lift from your legs. I know that, but I still couldn't do it.

Still, I was in my element. At least with a theory exam there are no opponents — apart from the book. Bring it on! I may not have swotted since my finals in 1983, but I know I can go one-on-one with a set text and come out victorious. However, there was still the fighting to get through.

My first fight was against the young teacher I'd met before. She only needed 10 points to get her black belt. I told her she wasn't getting them off me. (Rare burst of positive thinking.)

In the event, she got 7 of them. (Not quite positive enough.) Our fight went the full four minutes. She got me yet again early on with her drop-knee *seoi-nage*, but although she tried it repeatedly afterwards, I managed to ride it. My next fight was against the student I beat back at Easter. She'd had six months off with a broken finger she'd picked up that day. Our bout was over quickly, as I fell backwards attempting a half-hearted sacrifice throw — the one I'd spent so long practising — and she was awarded an *ippon*. We both stared at one another in surprise, knowing that she'd not really attempted a proper technique. So. Unlucky there. Never do a half-hearted sacrifice throw.

My third contest was as part of a line-up. If you're a right cow, being in a line-up is marginally more fun than an ordinary contest, because of the added incentive of preventing someone getting their dan grade. But for me that's irrelevant. None of it is fun. Our opponent was Karate Girl, a thuggish teen with a habit of oops! accidentally punching you in the face when getting a grip, or oops! kicking you in the leg while ostensibly attempting a foot sweep. And why not? Judo's a rough old sport. She got her black belt. The rest of us got the dotted imprint of her *gi* on our jaws.

Last fight. Nearly over. I was probably closer

to winning that one than any of them. At one point I swung her round in a full circle like a rag doll. If *only* I'd stuck a leg out, I'd probably have thrown her. It was so obvious to my mates watching. And to me looking back. But funny things happen when you're on the mat. The obvious is not what occurs to you. She won by a *waza-ari* throw, followed by yes! my good friend, *kesa gatame*. Twit. I assumed the throw was an *ippon*, so I just lay there and let her get the hold on. Schoolgirl error. It's not over till the fat lady lets out a blood-curdling *ki-ai*. Always carry on till the ref calls *Matte*. Instead, the next thing I heard was '*Osae-komi!*' (there's a hold on, start the clock) and I lay there thinking, *You silly bag.* I tried to get out, but no.

I'm disappointed, of course. But I fought better this time (apart from the being a twit aspect). Debbie agrees. She's says I've gone up to a whole new level, so I'm not utterly cast down. We were finished on our mat at around 11.15 a.m., but instead of going to catch the end of the service, I had to wait until there was a mat and an examiner free so that I could do my theory test. This wasn't until just after 2 p.m., long enough for exam nerves to kick in, but in the end it was fine. Heather is an excellent *uke*, making even my rubbish techniques look effective. And I seem to know my stuff. In fact, I was amazed at how much I already knew when I came to mug up. Osmosis, probably, from hanging around dojos.

So that was it. The grading was behind me again, which is where I like gradings to be, even if I've failed. It is not better to travel hopefully than arrive in this instance. It is better for it to be over. And one day it will be. Just keep on going.

7

Black Belt

O Jesus, I have promised
To serve thee to the end:
Be thou for ever near me,
My master and my friend;
I shall not fear the battle
If thou art by my side,
Nor wander from the pathway
If thou wilt be my guide.

Verse 1, Hymn 41
'O Jesus, I have promised'
in *With Cheerful Voice: Hymns for Children*

'O Jesus, I have promised' was popular at my primary school, even though we belonged to an era before the jazzy new tune came along. It remains popular with many people today, especially with those who aren't regular churchgoers, but who remember singing it at school with 'Morning has Broken' and 'The Lord of the Dance'. The only people who actively hate this hymn are bishops, because they are compelled to sing it at every single confirmation service they take. I heard of one bishop whose portrait was painted on his retirement. Someone remarked that it made him look rather miserable. 'It's my 'O Jesus, I have promised' face,' he explained dourly.

I expect I enjoyed this hymn because of its cheerful tune and the idea of Jesus as a friend who I was promising to serve 'to the end'. Little girls know all about promises of lifelong friendship. (We also liked the line in the last verse about 'my hope to follow Julie'.) Then there was the thrilling idea of The World as a sinful place, full of 'sights that dazzle' and 'tempting sounds'. The 'storms of passion' and 'murmurs of self-will' probably resonated with the gathering thunderclouds of puberty on the horizon. As a good chapelgoing child I prayed fervently that Jesus would shield my soul from sin; while secretly intending to get a jolly good look at it first.

These days I don't much care for 'O Jesus, I have promised'. (I've been to my share of confirmation services, too.) I have now sung the words to four different cheerful tunes, and in a spirit of fairness, I dislike them all equally. More importantly, I have a theological objection to the idea of The World as essentially sinful, and something from which all good evangelicals should therefore insulate themselves in a cosy Christian enclave, complete with Christian books and music. (And yo-yos.)

One phrase, however, remains potent, particularly when a grading is looming: 'My foes are ever near me, / Around me and within.' As my quest has gone on it has become increasingly clear that the foes around me — scary though they seem as we line up on the 1st kyu mat — are pussycats compared with the foes within. Of course, some of my opponents are ace fighters who will probably go on to represent their country. Fair play to them. But I am not overwhelmingly outclassed. Or I oughtn't to be. I'm big and strong, I'm experienced, my techniques are good. The problem is all in my mind: I am my own worst enemy.

Things came to a head in January of 2006, four weeks before a grading. I foolishly let myself think about it and I was overwhelmed by a surge of total dread. It felt as if I'd opened a window to my soul and the east wind had swept in. Try as I might, I couldn't get the thing shut again, or not for long. Whenever I accidentally thought about the prospect, I got the same ghastly set of feelings (realising you've misread the timetable and there's an exam tomorrow you haven't revised for, spotting your passport has expired the morning you are due to fly — this is the region we are talking about). I could tell that my fear was out of all proportion to the cause, and it occurred to me that a sports psychologist might be of help here, to advise me about such things as mental preparation, focus and whatever else sportspeople do to keep the east wind at bay.

Not really knowing how else to go about finding a sports psychologist, I asked one of Pete's old chums from his school cross-country team, Jack Buckner. It probably should have occurred to me that Jack, who competed in the Olympics and is a former European Games 5,000-metre champion, would be likely to have contacts a bit more high-powered than the nice hypnotherapist from Wolverhampton I'd been vaguely picturing. This is how I ended up having a one-to-one coaching session with the UK Athletics performance coach, Dave Collins. Pete's reaction was, 'Hey, wow, what a fantastic opportunity!' I must confess I experienced a tiny misgiving. Wasn't this rather like suddenly discovering your RE lesson was to be taken by the Archbishop of Canterbury?

I made my way to the UK Athletics headquarters (in a spanking new business park near Solihull) one bright morning in late January to meet Dave. He turned out to be a big bear of a man, bristling with qualifications (2nd dan judo, 3rd dan karate, ex-Royal Marines, PhD in psychology) and not hamstrung by a pathetic need to be liked. Perhaps this is just as well, given that his brief is — as I understand it — to drag the whole culture of athletics coaching into the twenty-first century and get zillions of gold medals for Britain. In the face of all his intimidating he-man qualifications, I was reassured to catch a blast of tremendous kindness coming off him.

After a bit of introductory banter — the visitor before me had left a purple scarf which Dave handed to an assistant, saying mincingly that it wasn't his colour — we got to business. First of all we clarified what I felt I needed — that I was trying to get my 1st dan, but thought that I lacked the ability to focus, and that some guidance with mental preparation would be useful. I described my feelings of acute dread. 'I suppose I just perceive gradings as . . . hostile.' He stared at me as if I were mad, and said, 'They *are* hostile.'

This was the moment when it first became obvious just how vast was the gulf between his experience of competitive sport and my own. He was inhabiting the stratosphere, while I occasionally cruised at rooftop altitude. But we pressed on, either because he was too kind to say 'For God's sake go home and bake cakes, woman!' or because he believed that the principles of sports psychology applied as much to me as to top-notch athletes. We sat side by side. On the desk in front of us was his laptop. He proposed that he talk me through a PowerPoint presentation which would address general questions of mental preparation, and after that, we'd talk more specifically about how I might prepare for judo gradings.

I can't remember exactly at which point I first burst into tears, but it may have been when he asked me, 'Why are you doing this to yourself?' Buggered if I know, I thought in sudden surprise. Instead I said — or rather squeaked in the way you do when you are trying not to cry — 'Because I want a black belt.' 'Go and buy one, then. Why are you putting yourself through this? You've got better things to do with your Sunday mornings. What are you trying to prove?'

It was like undergoing a mental acupressure session. I may have buttons that were left unpressed, but I can't think offhand what they might be. 'Can open, worms everywhere!' as Chandler once remarked in *Friends*. Clearly this landed Dave with a problem. He had signed up for a spot of coaching as a favour to a colleague, to see if it was possible, in a couple of hours, to transform a nervous vicar's wife into a focused killing machine. He wasn't expecting full-blown psychotherapy.

Funnily enough, none of it felt hostile. Probably because it wasn't. We limped on through the PowerPoint presentation — perceptions of pressure, cortisol and dopamine levels, fight or flight mechanism, stress as challenge not threat, stopping negative thoughts. I broke down repeatedly. Dave kept stopping to check that I was still OK with this. I kept assuring him I was. 'You know where all this is coming from, don't you?' 'Yes, from my childhood.' Among the many soul-baring things I blurted was, 'I want to be tough!' He took the view that if I was prepared to cry in front of a complete stranger like this, I *was* tough. I've thought about that since, and wonder if, deep down, I still adhere to my ten-year-old tomboy way of measuring toughness. Yet there I was, confronted by a man who possessed that kind of toughness in spades but who seemed to be using a different scale altogether.

We talked about focus. There is only this fight, just me and one opponent. Everything else is a distraction. 'Everything else' includes thoughts about the next fight, about the black belt, about other people's thoughts and feelings. It must be pure. Me or her. You can't hope simply to empty your mind of fear or negative thoughts. That's like trying not to think about elephants. Instead you must deliberately set those things aside and focus on what you intend to do: put your opponent on her back. I found myself remembering an awful occasion when I was driving down the A1 with my toddler smacking his baby brother in the back seat and the baby howling. At one point I actually turned right round to fend him off, yelling, 'Just stop that!' Then it occurred to me that there was no damage the two-year-old was capable of inflicting that came anywhere near to the damage I would do to the lot of us if I crashed. My one task was to focus on the road ahead, to block out everything else, calmly and repeatedly, until we were safely parked and I could yell to my heart's content.

In the days that remained before the grading I did my best to follow Dave's instructions, to banish negative thoughts, and replace them with positive ones, to welcome the stress I was feeling as a short-term surmountable challenge. It took considerable psychological energy but, as a game plan, it worked a lot better than blank terror partially blocked out by denial.

My first opponent was someone who'd beaten me in about ten seconds flat at a previous grading. Without the benefit of Dave's wisdom, it would have been over before we'd even stepped on the mat. I patiently silenced the foe within who kept prophesying I'd be killed just like last time. I replaced it with the mantra *This time it will be different. I will get the grip I want, and I will throw her.* The fight went nearly the full time. She won in the end, but I had her worried a couple of times. 'Wow, you've improved!' she said afterwards. She then proceeded to slaughter everyone else on the mat and get her black belt.

I had five more fights, and at no point did I just secretly give up. I was beaten easily by one young woman, but when I faced her a second time for her line-up, I thought, Right, you won't do that to me again. And she didn't. Admittedly, she did something else and won, but the point is, I was still focused, not downcast and longing to escape.

After it was all over I went back over to

where Debbie and Heather were sitting. For the third time I'd got no points from a grading. At the sight of my mates' sympathetic expressions I found I couldn't hang onto that focus for a moment longer. I felt it twang away from my grip like glider elastic. I rested my head on Debbie and wept. Then I said, 'Oh well,' and pulled myself back together. We talked it over. Basically I'd done well. Some of the fights had been very close. And I'd been unlucky with some of the refereeing decisions.[1]

By then the morning service was over, so Pete drove from church to collect me. I was coming down the stairs from the gallery area, and saw him walking in through a thicket of double takes. (Why is that bouncer dressed up as a vicar?) And I thought, now I was allowed to admit distractions again, how much, much more he means to me than any of this judo malarkey, how glad I am to have a life outside the dojo, and thank God it was all over for a few months. When I got back home, I saw the first nasty flicker of zigzaggy lights that precedes a migraine. I'd

---

[1] A so-called friend meanly pointed out that learning to blame the ref is a sure sign of sporting advancement.

held myself together so ruthlessly, I suppose it was inevitable.

* * *

That was the February grading in 2006. The finishing tape for my black-belt quest would be November of the same year, when I turned forty-five. I still needed 40 more points. A year earlier, when I'd just breezed my 1st kyu, the challenge of winning four fights would have seemed a complete doddle. But now there were only three more gradings left. Bloody hell. What if I wasn't going to make it after all? Given the way things were going, I was set to fail.

No! Banish those negative thoughts!

I tried, but I couldn't. With the benefit of hindsight it is now obvious to me why: I was depressed. This, I think, is the real reason why I wept so copiously over old Dave. Yes, he touched a few raw nerves, but like my dread at the prospect of gradings, the reaction was out of all proportion to the cause.

Depression had probably been creeping up on me for a long time. It was partly the time of year, partly the miscarriages, partly the horrible dragged-out employment tribunal and its fallout in the congregation.

This had left Pete emotionally exhausted. He was grappling with big decisions about his future ministry — was it time to move, or would that be cutting and running? Was applying for the post of canon at Lichfield Cathedral the next step, or not?

Parish ministry can be all-consuming. There are not enough hours in the day to meet the needs of all the parishioners. Priests are finite human beings. Knowing this does not prevent clergy, when they are at a low ebb, from looking around the congregation on a Sunday and thinking, I've let you down. I've failed you, too. And you, and you, and you. When guilt overwhelms your enthusiasm, ministry is no longer sustainable. It wasn't my job and my vocation, it was Pete's. The decision had to be his. But I felt sure it was time to leave.

It was not that I hated Walsall. How could I? To me it had represented a blessed escape. Good friends, lively church, nice schools, beautiful arboretum five minutes' stroll away. And a lovely house in a smart residential area with no bricks coming through my windows! (Unless they were thrown by my own children.) It wasn't Walsall's fault that it had ended up being the backdrop for the series of swingeing blows we ended up taking. By January of

2006, it felt as though there wasn't a single street or tree, or view from a window, or any corner of any room in the vicarage that wasn't tinged with my misery.

Combating this inner gloom was possible, in the way that it is possible to walk across a ploughed field at right angles to the furrows. I tried to be upbeat, to count my blessings, to make sure I went for a mood-lifting run most days. But no matter what I tried, things got worse. Everything seemed to make me cry. I was sleeping badly, jerking awake in panic most nights with my starving pet/Inland Revenue nightmare. I surfaced each morning under a haze of dread, which slowly lifted as the day wore on. Part of it was clearly hormonal (welcome to the decade of the peri-menopause!), but eventually it was blighting two weeks out of every four. Even an arithmaphobe like me could calculate that this was half my life. It took the unexpected trauma of my session with Dave to make me see that I needed to do something about it.

So I dug out my little Handbook for Desperate Clergy Wives, and found myself a counsellor. The diocese offers a certain number of free sessions to clergy and their spouses, recognising the stresses peculiar to vicarage life. Or maybe with an eye to the fact that counselling is cheaper than my running amok and burning the church down. When I confided my decision to a friend, her response was, 'I won't say I told you so.' Good, I thought, then I won't smack you one. Members of the congregation seemed, annoyingly, to have diagnosed my condition before I'd got there myself.

Over the following couple of months I made my way regularly to a house in a little Staffordshire village to talk to my counsellor, until it seemed to both of us that we had run out of useful things to discuss, and I was on the mend. The process shed some light on why I react as I do in certain situations, and gave me some strategies for coping. As I look back, those months seem grey and blurry in my memory, like endless rainy streets in a February belonging to somebody else's life. It would have been nice simply to fast-forward to the day we arrived here in Lichfield and I began to feel like my old self again. Attractive though the idea is, it would mean missing a couple of important issues which (like a true judo player) I wrestled with doggedly. Both of them, interestingly, turned out to be things that Dave pressed me about during our lachrymose PowerPoint session.

The first is this: What am I trying to

prove? Why am I so driven? Why do I set myself a target, then hold myself to it as if I had taken a sacred vow, and will have to sacrifice my firstborn if I renege on the deal? 'For how long after you got your PhD were you satisfied?' Dave asked me at one point. He admitted that his sense of satisfaction lasted about ten minutes. While mine lasted longer than that, a doctorate no longer feels like the big deal it appeared to be all those years I was working towards it. So what drives people like us to carry on and on proving ourselves? Who are we trying to prove it to? Where is this coming from? From our childhood. Dave told me about a card he'd had from his father, shortly before he died, which said how proud and grateful he was. At this point it was Dave, not me, teetering on the brink of tears. (Which, of course, made me cry too.)

My parents are proud of me. I've asked them. But when I was a child they didn't come out with it very often, because to articulate your pride in your children felt like boasting, and my mother came from the kind of background where people were discouraged from getting above themselves. Unlike other adults, Mum and Dad never made it their mission to cut me down to size. Inadvertently, though, they gave me the impression that nothing I ever achieved really counted for anything, because it was more important to be kind and good. This was further complicated by the fact that I did better at school than my big sister, so they were understandably cagey about making much fuss of my success. Well, obviously, I was obliged to draw attention to my brilliance. This is why I'm so driven: I've spent my whole life effectively jumping up and down shouting, 'Look at me! Notice me! Aren't I clever?'

Held in tension with this imperative to be brilliant was the message of my Nonconformist Chapel upbringing, which stressed the futility of trying to achieve anything, because even our righteousness is as filthy rags in God's sight. Nothing you can conceivably do will ever impress God, because we are all hell-deserving sinners. But the catch was this: if you didn't read your Bible and go to Sunday school, and were bad instead (e.g. saying 'bum' and 'bloody', telling fibs and pinching people), it was a sure sign that you hadn't invited the Lord Jesus into your heart properly, *that you weren't really a Christian at all.* If you died, you would go to hell. Simple as that. I have moved a long way from my earliest theological position, but it seems that underneath there remains, way down, a bedrock of dread. *The Second Coming might happen before I'm ready, and I'll be left behind.*[1]

The other matter that I ended up confronting in counselling was my tendency to bury my head in the sand. Dave had no time for this kind of weakness. At one point I suspect he wanted to shake me till my teeth rattled. He was trying to help me categorise the different types of opponent I might encounter (fridge woman, psycho teen, and so on), and to decide on the most effective strategy to employ against them. I feebly told him I couldn't bear to think about it. In exasperation he snapped that there was no other area of my life where I would operate like this. 'If your husband said one day, 'Oh, by the way, I've invited the bishop and fifty other clergy for dinner tonight,' you wouldn't just sit there wringing your hands saying, 'Oh

---

[1] There is also much about my childhood experience of Christianity that I am grateful for: my knowledge of the Bible, the kindly presence in my life of many, many constant and good-hearted adults; an understanding that faith is about a relationship with God; and, not least, my compendium of interesting and useful hymns.

I hope it will all be OK.' You'd get on and sort it!'

Just between you and me, Dave was wrong. Not about mass catering at short notice, I can do that, but about there being no other area of my life where I'd operate like an ostrich. I'm like it about Her Majesty's Revenue and Customs. I was like it about exams. At Durham I could never bear to make a revision timetable in case it revealed I didn't have enough time to revise everything. I'm scared of cocking things up and failing, so scared I put things off till the last minute, then skitter about trying to cover every possible base without ever confronting the problem squarely. I wake in the night in a cold sweat. It goes back to my childhood fire-and-brimstone fear, that if you make one mistake, you're done for.

It strikes me that, rather brilliantly, I have chosen a sport with the same mechanism built into it: one mistake and you're out. *Ippon*. Match over. No arguments, no excuses. Fortunately, that's not all there is to judo. You may have just lost, but there will be other matches. You are allowed to pick yourself up and have another go. The long-term process is merciful, even if each individual episode feels ruthless. Maybe judo is teaching me to believe that life is also like this. You're allowed to make mistakes. It's not the end of the world. Just get over yourself.

What I don't know is whether I would have tied myself into such anguished knots over all this if I hadn't been suffering from depression. The saddest thing of all was that, until then, judo had always been one of my coping mechanisms. It switched from being part of the solution to being part of the problem. In my role as my own worst enemy, I'd transformed the challenge of getting a black belt from a stiffish climb into an assault on Everest.

★ ★ ★

Horrible, horrible, horrible.

So. What can I do to jack up the pressure and make it *even more horrible* for myself? Why, I could always miss the next two gradings so that everything depended on the very last one! That wasn't actually my plan, but two separate injuries — a broken toe in February and torn quad muscles in July — ensured that this was how it ended up. Even without the injuries. I would have struggled to achieve the right sort of focus and the appropriate level of training. We were in the throes of moving house with all the ghastliness that entails: furtling through the junk in the loft, driving to the tip, sorting out new schools, chiselling the fossilised fat off the kitchen units, saying our farewells.

But eventually it was all done, and here we are in Lichfield. And so it was that on the morning of Sunday 12 November 2006, eight days before my forty-fifth birthday, I got in the car and headed back to Walsall for my last grading. It was a glorious sunny day. The gardens were still full of summer flowers as I drove out of Lichfield. Handel's *Dixit Dominus* was playing. I was scared as usual, but somehow resigned. If I won a few fights, great, I'd carry on. If not, I could honourably give up. It was a win-win situation, I told myself.

There was quite a gang of us on the 'ladies' 1st kyu mat. Some I recognised, others were strangers. I approached one and asked if she was a fellow veteran. 'Yes, I'm thirty-seven!' she said proudly, in the way we women of a certain age tend to do, hoping the other person will reel back in astonishment. I hadn't even *started* judo when I was thirty-seven, I thought. I knew she'd be my first opponent, and she was. I fought well, using a double-lapel grip, which annoys people, but she still won.

My second fight was against the young woman who'd beaten me twice at the previous grading. It was a tough fight. At one stage I was winning with a *waza-ari*, but didn't realise. I threw her again, and she twisted and landed on her face, crying, 'My nose!' Instantly, I paused, put a hand on her thigh and asked, 'Are you OK?' Keith, Debbie and Heather were dancing in frustration. That was the point where I should have tried to finish her off. The ref called *matte*, and gave her time to recover. She got up and threw me. *Ippon.*

Then there was a long wait while the judges sorted out the line-ups. As I stood beside the mat, my mood changed abruptly. Sudden dismay, as if I'd witnessed something appalling. A strange taste filled my mouth like sour blood. What's happening to me? I thought in panic. I've got to get out! Keith was there. He explained to the senior referee. I officially withdrew and was escorted to the medical room. Heather came and sat with me. Gradually I calmed down. I drank a cup of tea and began to feel like a fraud. It was like skiving off PE in matron's.

So that was it. It was done. I leaned my head back against the wall. It had ended almost literally with a whimper. Tears leaked from my closed eyes. Then the zigzaggy lights started up. Another migraine. It was an unmistakable distress flare from my subconscious. Stop! For the love of God, stop doing this! We are not enjoying it!

When my vision cleared, I drove back home. My family were there waiting for me. I told them what had happened, how I'd had to withdraw, and that by doing so I'd prevented several others from getting their line-up. They hugged me. 'Never mind, Mum,' my older son said. 'Look at it this way: you may have failed, but you took down three other women with you.' We sat at the kitchen table having lunch and I looked around at them groggily. Well, here I still am. I can live with it.

I tried to sleep off the rest of the migraine, but it was Remembrance Day and the cathedral bells were pealing about eighty yards from my bedroom window. So I got up and went to evensong. I sat next to Pete up in the choir, in the stall the vergers reserve for Mrs Chancellor. Psalm 46: 'God is our hope and strength: a very present help in trouble. Therefore will we not fear, though the earth be moved: and though the hills be carried into the midst of the sea . . . He maketh wars to cease in all the world . . . Be still then, and know that I am God.' The choir sang Bainton's anthem 'And I saw a New Heaven', with its vision, from the end of the book of Revelation, of the new age where there will be no more weeping and pain. 'Roll on that day,' I mumbled to Glenn, a member of the choir, as we left the cathedral after the service. 'Yes, but not *too* quickly,' he replied, 'because I'm still rather enjoying this life.' (He's from New Zealand.)

★ ★ ★

That night, as I tried to unwind enough to sleep, I went over the whole thing in my mind. Why had I done this to myself? Had it been worth it?

If nothing else, I was now sporty. 'You are an example to us all,' the dean had said a month before (in the tone of a man who would rather kneel on carpet tacks than go running). I'd toughened up. I was physically less timid. Earlier that week I'd been trying to visit the library, but the entrance was blocked by two large teenage lads wrestling. Instead of feebly finding an alternative route, I carried on. They shifted, one of them saying mockingly, 'Mind the lady!' Ha. The lady could dump you on your sorry backside without dropping her library books, sonny.

I'd toughened up mentally too. By going to all those gradings I'd proved I had the guts to put myself repeatedly in the situation I most loathed and dreaded; like someone phobic about public speaking volunteering over and over to do the best man's speech. And in a more low-key way I'd been shaped by the week in, week out discipline of training, of making myself drive to Wolverhampton on a winter night when I'd rather stay in and drink wine. There's nothing like pegging away at something for months and years to cure you of the idea that you deserve something for nothing *because you're worth it*. And there's nothing like failure to combat society's other big myth — that if you only *believe* in yourself and give it 100 per cent, you can become anything you want.

You can't. We can't all be champions. I will go on encouraging my sons not to be quitters, I tell myself, and to carry on fighting the good fight and running the straight race. But I also want them to know that there are times when it's all right to call it a day; that human worth isn't all bound up in achievements. (Not that they ever thought it was. Only that morning my younger son had reassured me he'd still love me if I didn't win.)

So, yes. Yes, it was worth it. But was it really over? After all, there's nothing stopping you having another go, is there? — that's what people were going to say. True, part of me would always be sad I never made 1st dan. But a far larger part was singing hallelujah at the thought of never, ever having to go to another grading. Pain is temporary, quitting lasts for ever — at least, I jolly well hope it does.

Some things are denied us in this life. Thank God for people who love us unconditionally, for family and good friends. Because that's the other thing I've gained — a new set of mates who care how I'm doing both on the mat and off it, and who respect me (when they aren't taking the piss). It's a club that can produce champions, but one that also has time for losers. So I knew that when I reappeared at the club next week — quest over, no black belt — it would all be fine. In a way, nothing much would have changed. I'd still be training with the ones I'd met right at the beginning — Keith and Debbie and Heather and Lloyd — but also with a whole bunch of new friends. The only difference would be that now I could do judo for judo's own sake. Just for the sheer hell of it.

As I finally drifted off to sleep, head still jangling, every limb aching, I thought again about the old hymn. I decided, on the whole, that I liked the last verse best:

Faint not nor fear, his arms are near,
He changeth not, and thou art dear;

Only believe, and thou shalt see
That Christ is all in all to thee.

Over the next couple of days the aches eased and the dust settled. You know what? I've decided that inner foe was a friend after all. It was saying: You don't have to do this to yourself, Catherine. You have nothing to prove. Just be a brown belt. Enjoy judo. Enjoy life. What is a black belt, anyway? Remember it's just a white belt blackened with years of dirt. And when you've had your black belt long enough it will start to wear out, and the white underneath will begin to show through — that's what they say in martial arts. It's all one big circle. It means nothing.

In the end it came down to this: I wanted it too much in the wrong way, and not enough in the right way. I wanted so desperately to be a black belt that I made the task impossible for myself. But I didn't want it enough to change and become a focused and ruthless killing machine. When my opponent lands on her face, my reflex is compassion — I kind of like that about myself.

A few days after the grading I went for a run. It was a perfect morning. As I trotted along the Close looking up at the cathedral spires against the impossible blue of the sky, I thought: I'll never have to go to a grading again. In few days I'll be forty-five. It's done. Life is good.

Then I tripped and went headlong. At the last moment I managed to turn and execute a rolling breakfall on the tarmac of the close. Twit! Then I got up, rubbed the blood and grit off my hands, and ran three miles in the November sunshine anyway.

Acknowledgements

My thanks to everyone who helped and supported me, both on and off the mat, while I was writing this book. Firstly, I'd like to say a big thank you to everyone I've ever trained with, because I'm truly grateful. And because it would be unwise to annoy any of them by failing to give them a mention. In particular, I'd like to thank my mates at Oak Park, Wolverhampton Youth Judo and Lichfield Judo clubs; not forgetting the good folk at the Wellington Judo and Jujitsu Academy, especially Cameron, who made me so welcome during my months in New Zealand. Most of all, my thanks go to my coaches — Keith Jones, Debbie Cox and Heather Manser — for all their expertise, good humour, patience and friendship over the last few years. And to Dee, for accepting my subs each week, even when she knows I've raided the charity box.

I am very grateful to my parents, family and friends, and to the congregations of St Paul's Church at the Crossing, Walsall, and Lichfield Cathedral. I am not a normal clergy wife, and you have been very tolerant. Thanks to Tristan Jones at Yellow Jersey for his encouragement and micro-editing, and to my agent, Anthony Goff, for spurring me on by telling me what a bad idea this was, but even more for supporting me when I went ahead with it anyway. And to Richard, who told me so.

Last of all, and most importantly, a heartfelt thank you to Pete, Jonathan and Tom, for loving me whether I win or lose.

We do hope that you have enjoyed reading this large print book.

Did you know that all of our titles are available for purchase?

We publish a wide range of high quality large print books including:
**Romances, Mysteries, Classics
General Fiction
Non Fiction and Westerns**

Special interest titles available in large print are:
**The Little Oxford Dictionary
Music Book
Song Book
Hymn Book
Service Book**

Also available from us courtesy of Oxford University Press:
**Young Readers' Dictionary
(large print edition)
Young Readers' Thesaurus
(large print edition)**

For further information or a free brochure, please contact us at:
**Ulverscroft Large Print Books Ltd.,
The Green, Bradgate Road, Anstey,
Leicester, LE7 7FU, England.
Tel:** (00 44) 0116 236 4325
Fax: (00 44) 0116 234 0205